Voices in Time

A NEW WINDMILL BOOK OF LITERARY NON-FICTION

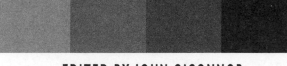

EDITED BY JOHN O'CONNOR

Heinemann
New Windmills

Heinemann is an imprint of Pearson Education Limited, a company incorporated in England and Wales having its registered office at Edinburgh Gate, Harlow, Essex, CM20 2JE Registered company number: 872828

Heinemann is a registered trademark of Pearson Educational Limited

12

ISBN: 978 0 435125 24 0

Cover design by The Point

Photographs: Rex Features, p.2; Rex Features, p.17; BBC Photo Library, p.35; Rex Features, p.53; Rex Features, p.75; Hulton Getty, p.80; Rex Features, p.113; Rex Features, p.143; Peter Newark's American Pictures, p.148; Rex Features, p.167

Cover photographs: Marilyn Monroe, Camera Press/Cecil Beaton; David Beckham, Empics Ltd/Barry Coombs; Nelson Mandela, Popperfoto

Typeset by 🟋 Tek-Art, Croydon, Surrey

Printed in China (CTPSC/12)

CONTENTS

INTRODUCTION FOR TEACHERS

Meeting curriculum requirements

Voices in Time has been designed to meet the requirements of the National Curriculum for English to introduce pupils to 'non-fiction and non-literary texts', including:

'a) literary non-fiction
b) print and ICT-based information and reference texts
c) media and moving image texts.'

(The National Curriculum for England: English; 2000)

Differentiation is provided through the subject matter (from David Beckham in the opening section to Charles Dickens); the ascending difficulty of language (from a wide-appeal sports book to a literary biography) and in the activities themselves.

A focus on genre

The extracts have been arranged according to genre. This is to enable students to study the art of letter writing across the centuries, say, or to compare a variety of different approaches to autobiography. Each section is then followed by activities which end with a comparative task which enables the students to revise and use what they have learned. The concluding section offers the opportunity to follow the record of a great man's life in a variety of genres from children's encyclopedias to letters published in newspapers.

I hope that you will find that *Voices in Time* is a valuable resource in helping to meet the non-fiction requirements for all your Key Stage 3 students.

John O'Connor

INTRODUCTION FOR STUDENTS

The extracts in this book all come under the heading of 'non-fiction'. Unlike novels and short stories, which are made up ('fiction'), these are true stories about real people. Captain Scott really did die in his attempt to be the first to reach the South Pole and the diary entries you can read here were written by him during his last days.

But not all the extracts are about life-and-death dramas. You can find out how Claire Danes and Leonardo DiCaprio got on while they were filming together, or how nervous Robbie Williams gets before his performances.

The activities at the end of each section help you explore the extracts in more depth and find new ways of looking at them both separately and by comparing them with each other. In doing them, you will also learn about some of the most fascinating kinds of non-fiction that people have produced over the centuries: biographies, autobiographies, diaries, letters and speeches.

I hope you enjoy reading these extracts. You'll move from laughing at Clive James's childhood in Australia to reading the story of Nelson Mandela and the great changes in South Africa. In between you'll meet familiar and unknown people – but I hope you will be fascinated by them all.

John O'Connor

Section 1

BIOGRAPHY

A biography is a piece of writing about someone's life. Some biographers give you a person's complete life story (as Peter Ackroyd does with Charles Dickens). Others focus on a particular episode in a person's life (as Grace Catalano does here when she writes about the first meeting between Claire Danes and Leonardo DiCaprio).

It can take years to write a successful biography: hours of patient research and careful weighing of evidence. Even then, when the book is finally published, many readers will claim that you have got it wrong, because it is biased or fails to present a true picture. Was David Beckham a hero or a villain, for example, when he got himself sent off in an important World Cup match? And what were Paul McCartney's real feelings when he heard of fellow-Beatle John Lennon's death?

David Beckham
Mark Palmer

It is 1998 and the England football team are expected to do well in the World Cup. One of their star players is David Beckham. In the second round they meet their old rivals Argentina. At half-time the scores are level and English hopes are high. But three minutes after the interval an incident occurs which is to change everything . . .

Beckham hadn't touched the ball in the second half when Simeone crashed into him. He was spread-eagled on the ground, Simeone patted him on the head for the benefit of the referee, who was standing four yards away. Suddenly, Beckham jerked his right foot up and his heel struck Simeone behind his knee. It was as if his leg was on a pulley being operated by some sinister character hidden deep within the stadium. The kick wasn't hard – from that position it couldn't be – and it didn't hurt Simeone, but the Argentinian captain went down clutching at various parts of his leg as if amputation was imminent. The Argentinians crowded round Nielsen, who put his hand in his pocket and began fishing for a card. Shearer feared the worst and waved the meddling Argentinians away. The referee called Beckham towards him and showed him a yellow one, but then his hand went back into the pocket and came back out with red. Beckham looked back only once, briefly, as he walked off. By the time he reached the touchline he had untucked his shirt and his eyes were watering up. He didn't look at Hoddle and Hoddle didn't look at him. But Batistuta smiled.

With the scores level after extra time, the game has to be settled by penalties. Each team has to select five players to take the penalties, but several of England's best penalty-takers are no longer on the field and some inexperienced players will have to be chosen.

When Nielsen blew, Hoddle went first to Owen. He was eighteen years old and he was about to take a penalty for his country in front of a television audience of more than 24 million in England alone. Owen went to talk to

Shearer. Seaman gulped from a plastic bottle and shook Adams by the hand. Ince paced up and down, joking nervously with his friend McManaman. Campbell was having his calves massaged. Overall, England looked the more confident. The Argentinians were flopped on the ground, shattered. A list was handed to the referee with the names of the first five penalty-takers and the order in which they would be taken.

The goalkeepers shook hands and walked towards the end occupied entirely by Argentinians. Sergio Berti went with them. He put the ball down and hit it firmly past Seaman. 1–0. Shearer came forward. You could tie yourself in knots thinking about it. Shearer had already taken one penalty. Should he put it in the same place? It might be sensible for him to aim for a different spot, but then the goalkeeper would have worked that out and so why not go for the same place after all? But then the goalkeeper knew that Shearer knew what the goalkeeper knew. The best thing would be to strike it so that even if he dived the right way he could never get near it. Which is what Shearer did. 1–1.

Hernan Crespo walked towards Seaman. One of the substitutes. Only twenty-two years old. Seaman dived to his left and saved it. The England fans let out a roar. For the first time since Beckham was sent off, England were in front. Surely, one more save from Seaman would clinch it and then on to Marseille for a second time. Owen would be next. But Owen wasn't next. Nor was Merson. It was Paul Ince.

Ince bounced the ball twice on his way to the penalty area, and as he put it down his eyes darted about like they had done four months earlier in his car outside Liverpool's training ground. 'If it means going to take a penalty, then I will have to take one,' he had said. He hit it with the inside of his right foot and Roa saved.

Then Veron scored. You knew he would. It was Merson's turn. Roa was off his line, but when the referee told him to get back he began complaining that the ball wasn't properly on the spot. Merson picked it up and bounced it a few times while the referee showed Roa a yellow card. But it didn't put Merson off. He stayed on his plimsolls and scored. It was 2–2 with two to go. Marcelo Gallardo, another substitute, scored his, and then came Owen. Six months ago he was turning up at England training sessions for work experience and was too young to buy a drink in a pub. He hardly looked at the goal. He just thumped the ball and it hit the inside of the post before ricocheting into the net. Owen turned round and rubbed his hands together.

Seaman would have to save the next one. But Ayala's penalty was too good. Advantage Argentina. It was down to David Batty to keep England in the World Cup finals. He looked confident enough, but he had never taken a penalty in his life, never scored a goal of any kind for England. People used to joke that Batty didn't even know how to play a forward pass. Beckham was watching from inside the tunnel. Behind me and to the left, Brian Moore was asking Kevin Keegan whether Batty would do it. 'Yes or no?' said Moore. 'Yes,' said Keegan. Batty missed. England had lost in France.

Many people blamed David Beckham for the defeat, feeling that, if he hadn't been sent off, things would have been very different. But the England manager Glenn Hoddle refused to go that far: 'I'm not here to blame an individual,' he said. 'He will be back in four years' time for another World Cup and he simply has to learn that you cannot do that sort of thing.' In the next round Argentina lost to Holland.

Ewan McGregor
Brian Pendreigh

When Brian Pendreigh wrote this biography, the actor Ewan McGregor had just become famous as the young Obi-Wan Kenobi in the *Star Wars* prequel, *The Phantom Menace*. But what made him want to be an actor in the first place? One answer lies in a childhood visit to the cinema to see Uncle Denis piloting an X-wing fighter alongside Luke Skywalker . . .

George Lucas's *Star Wars* may have been just a movie to some. But it was *the* defining moment in the lives of two little Scottish boys, nine-year-old Colin McGregor and his cheeky-faced wee brother Ewan. Little did they know it then, but *Star Wars* would shape their futures and determine the course of their adult lives.

Star Wars was an adventure film set in outer space, with aliens and robots and high-tech light-sabres, but at heart it is also a gloriously old-fashioned battle between Good and Evil, offering moral certainty in a world of turmoil and increasing moral ambivalence. *Star Wars* opened in the United States in the spring of 1977, but it was not until the end of that year that it was released in London, by which time it was already the highest-grossing film ever. The people of Tayside, where Colin and Ewan McGregor lived, would have to wait another couple of months before the film finally made it to their screens.

Even before its world première, Colin and Ewan had thirsted for information about Princess Leia, Luke Skywalker, Hans Solo and Obi-Wan Kenobi. From Rochdale to Rio, kids all over the world were desperate to see *Star Wars* and join in the adventure. But Colin and Ewan had an extra reason to look forward to seeing the movie. Their uncle was in it.

Although Denis Lawson is probably best known for his role as the hotel-keeper Urquhart, in Bill Forsyth's lyrical comedy-drama *Local Hero*, he was in all three of the original *Star Wars* movies, playing the role of Wedge. His nephews would see him pilot an X-wing fighter plane and do battle with the forces of the evil Galactic Empire, along with Luke Skywalker.

Uncle Denis, Ewan's mother's brother, had always been a highly exotic element in the life of the McGregor boys. Like his nephews, he had grown up in Perthshire. But now he lived in a galaxy far, far away, called London. Whenever he came back to Perthshire for a visit, he stood out from the locals as surely as Darth Vader would at a Women's Guild coffee morning. Other local men wore business suits or functional waxed jackets and welly boots. Long-haired Denis dressed in sheepskin waistcoats, beads and sandals. Ewan says that Denis actually handed out flowers in the High Street to bemused passers-by, but it may be that Ewan's memory – or his sense of humour – is playing tricks. One thing was certain however – Denis was different. And Ewan, who already liked nothing better than to attract attention, was excited by that difference.

Ewan was not exactly sure what an actor was, but he did know that actors did not have to be just one person, like everybody else, but got to be a whole series of people in turn – like children in a game. And people – children and grown-ups – would come to see them do it; they would watch and they would applaud. The McGregor family had already seen Denis at Perth Theatre. He had been Simple Simon in *Babes in the Wood* – though Ewan himself was just a babe then – and had been Able in *Robinson*

Crusoe. On one occasion Denis even called the boys up on stage. But *Star Wars* was something else entirely, *Star Wars* was a film, and Uncle Denis would be up there, larger than life, splashed right across the cinema screen in glorious Technicolor.

Colin and Ewan lived with their parents, Carol and Jim, in the town of Crieff, 18 miles outside Perth. Its imposing old stone villas, **hydropathic hotel** and boarding school nestle between the River Earn and the foothills of the Scottish Highlands. Crieff is a quiet little town built on history and tradition, where the siting of a new bus stop is front-page news in the *Strathearn Herald*; the sort of town which, in an age of increasing automation, still employs a human attendant at the public toilets in the town square.

The trip to see *Star Wars* at the Odeon cinema in Perth was to be a grand family outing, a birthday treat for Colin, as well as a celebration of Denis's elevation to the big time. Included in the party were Denis's parents – Ewan's grandparents – who had a jeweller's shop in Crieff High Street, and Denis's granny, Ewan's great-grandmother. The excitement of the big day was such that, even years later, as a full-grown man, Ewan can remember the feeling of anticipation, standing outside school, waiting to be picked up. The short car journey between Crieff and Perth seemed to take forever, but at last they were there, installed in their seats, waiting for the house lights to dim and the big picture to begin. The popcorn and Kia-Ora had been bought, the adverts had run their course and a buzz of excitement ran around the cinema as the opening prologue scrolled upwards and drifted off into the far reaches of space.

Those opening words 'A long time ago in a galaxy far, far away . . .' have become part of cinema legend. Although

hydropathic hotel: a hotel where people who are ill stay in order to be cured with the help of the local water

the six-year-old Ewan was too young to follow the written account of the war between the Galactic Empire and the rebels, he was swept up, from the start, in the colour and flow of the film. Like countless millions around the world he was charmed by the comedy of the opening scene between C-3PO, the paranoid android, forever bemoaning his lot, and his little chum R2-D2, who looks like a metal dustbin and communicates in a series of electronic beeps. There was a princess called Leia; heroes called Luke Skywalker and Han Solo; a menagerie of strange space creatures; Darth Vader, a wheezing villain encased in black; and a strange old man by the name of Obi-Wan Kenobi.

Carried along by the action, Colin and Ewan barely had time to wonder when Uncle Denis would appear on screen . . . which is just as well, as he does not turn up until the climactic aerial battle, when a squadron of X-wing fighters speed in formation towards the huge Death Star, which looks more like a metal moon than a spacecraft. 'Look at the size of that thing,' gasps Uncle Denis, in pilot's orange overalls and matching visor, behind the controls of one of the aircraft. The action is fast and furious as the aerial combat begins, cutting between Luke Skywalker and Uncle Denis and the other pilots. When Luke is unable to shake an enemy TIE fighter off his tail, Uncle Denis comes to his rescue, blasts the pursuer and saves him. Luke pilots his fighter into the Death Star itself, with the spirit of Obi-Wan Kenobi coolly, oh-so-coolly, urging him to 'use the Force' rather than his electronic targeting device. He fires his torpedoes into the exhaust port and turns the Death Star into a supernova.

Luke Skywalker saves the universe. And all because Uncle Denis had saved Luke Skywalker. It is a pity, then, that Lucasfilm spelt Denis's name wrongly on the credits – sticking an extra 'n' in Denis – and that they felt it necessary to have another actor to rerecord his lines in an American accent, but these were more the sort of details that a mother might worry about rather than his adoring nephews. And his character was one of the few fighter pilots to survive the combat, enabling him to return in the sequels.

'I decided to become an actor,' says Ewan, 'even though I had no idea what that meant.'

He would find out. In due course he would take up the light-sabre, and star in the next generation of *Star Wars* movies. And his brother Colin? He too was inspired by his Uncle's example. Colin joined the Royal Air Force.

Two little boys went to the pictures and saw their uncle acting the part of a fighter pilot. One little boy became an actor and the other little boy became a fighter pilot.

Claire Danes and Leonardo DiCaprio
Grace Catalano

When director Baz Luhrmann decided to make a new film version of Shakespeare's *Romeo and Juliet*, he looked around for the ideal pairing to play the 'star-crossed lovers'. He quickly cast Leonardo DiCaprio as Romeo, but then began a world-wide search for Juliet. Day after day, DiCaprio would act out the same scenes with different actresses keen to get the part; but for a long time there did not seem to be anyone suitable . . .

When Claire Danes came in, both Leonardo and Luhrmann knew they had found Juliet. 'She was strong with Leonardo,' says Luhrmann.

Leonardo also praised Claire's audition. 'She was the only one who came up and said the words directly to me,' he says. 'It was a little shocking, but it impressed me because most of the other girls auditioning looked off into the sky. Claire was right there, in front of my face, saying every line with power.'

Actually, it was no surprise that Claire Danes won the role. She is, after all, the best young actress to emerge from Hollywood in a long time. She first gained attention as Angela on the critically acclaimed TV series *My So-Called Life*. The show didn't last long, but Claire's performance was recognized with an Emmy nomination and a Golden Globe Award for Best Actress in a television drama.

Claire quickly moved into films, making her feature debut as Beth in the 1994 version of *Little Women* with Winona Ryder. In only two years, Claire has been in the films *How to Make an American Quilt, Home for the Holidays*, and *To Gillian on Her 37th Birthday*.

Claire was excited to learn she would be playing Juliet, saying the role 'is remarkable because she [Juliet] is determined and mature, but at the same time, she has an innocence to her, a youth and a freshness. She is very thoughtful, smart and passionate. She is an incredibly modern character who makes her own decisions and takes fate into her own hands.'

The flame that smoldered between Leonardo and Claire was obvious from the first day they worked together. John Leguizamo, who plays the villainous Tybalt in the film, says of his two costars, 'I think they had crushes on each other but they kept it very professional. Nothing was ever done. And that's great, because when you consummate an attraction you totally defuse the tension on the screen.'

Luhrmann was thrilled with the electricity between Leonardo and Claire. He says, 'One thing that I have absolutely no doubt about in this film is their onscreen chemistry. It's the sort of thing that's so defined. You can have two fantastic actors and still, the moment you see them onscreen, it's either there or it's not. They absolutely had it. And as it turned out, Leonardo and Claire were like brother and sister on the set.'

There was no denying that they got along, but flare-ups did occur. They spent so much time together that there was some tension between them.

'There were arguments. They went through some very difficult times emotionally on the set. There were definitely times when all three of us sniped at each other,' Luhrmann admits. 'Sometimes Leo and Claire were like two kids on holiday and sometimes it was like you were dragging your children through a desert and they were starving and suffering. But because they were so young and in the middle of such extraordinary events, I think they came to rely on each other, which was a great thing to behold.'

Before the filming of *William Shakespeare's Romeo + Juliet*, Luhrmann had Leonardo and Claire rehearse extensively. He wanted to be sure they understood the characters and the language. 'When he [Leonardo] arrived the first time, I really didn't know how he would handle the language,' says Luhrmann. 'After the initial read-through, we went through the text thoroughly and deliberately and when we went back to it, the words just came out of his mouth as if it were the most natural language possible. To me, the language in Leonardo's mouth is a wonderful thing to hear because the words have resonance. He speaks them as if they really are his words, and that's something you don't always get in a Shakespearean performance.'

'One of our main themes was clarity,' says Claire. 'During rehearsal, when Baz and Leo and I were working out what we were going to do, we did an exercise where we were absolutely literal. For every word we said, we'd find a way to make it clear with our hands. It was a little corny and we felt ridiculous doing it, but it really emphasized the idea that you can never be too obvious, precise, and clear with the language.'

There were times when Claire didn't know how she was going to read the classic Shakespearean lines and bring new life to them. 'I was sitting there about to go and do the famous balcony scene, and I was, like, "What am I about to do? I'm about to say, 'O, Romeo, Romeo! Wherefore art thou Romeo?' ",' she says. 'And I'm thinking, "This is a joke, right? How am I going to do this in a fresh way?".'

To say Leonardo was nervous about performing Shakespeare's language is an understatement. It didn't come easy to him at all. He wasn't sure, at first, how to play Romeo. 'I thought I would have to put on an English accent and try a sort of Affected Shakespeare Thing,' he says. 'But Baz explained that he wanted to make it very understandable and clear, and after working with him awhile, I began to feel more comfortable with it. There is a lot of beauty in each word and when I began to dissect sentences, I'd find meanings referring to something way back in the script, or words with double and triple meanings. So I really had to know what I was talking about to do the words justice. But at the same time, I had to make it conversational. That was a challenge and different from anything I'd ever done – and I liked it.'

Paul McCartney
Ross Benson

During their time with the Beatles, Paul McCartney and John Lennon became one of the most famous and successful song-writing partnerships in music history. But, when news came of Lennon's sudden and violent death, McCartney simply could not find the right words.

John Lennon was gunned down outside his home in the Dakota building at seven minutes past eleven on the evening of 8 December 1980, and became a myth and a martyr.

Paul McCartney's first reaction to his death was one of shocked bewilderment. Irritation came later. For in dying so violently, so senselessly, Lennon had forever claimed the glorious immortality in which McCartney dearly wanted to share. He was at home in the small house in Sussex that the McCartney family made their English base when his office telephoned him with the news of Lennon's murder. It was early in the morning, British time, and Linda was out taking the children to school.

'It was all blurred,' he recalled. 'You couldn't take it in.' He responded by sticking to the banality of his ordinary routine and went to the recording studio in London where he was working. 'Nobody could stay home with that news,' he explained. 'We just had to keep going. So I went in and did a day's work in a kind of shock.'

That evening, as he was leaving, a reporter asked him how he felt. He replied, 'It's a drag.' It was a trite answer that has dogged him ever since, and cast him irretrievably as glib and insensitive. Words had failed the songwriter in speech, as they sometimes did in song.

'I meant drag in the heaviest sense of the word – you know. It's a *drag*,' he explained later, though conceding that, in hard type, it did look too 'matter of fact'. It had been the same when his mother died and he asked, insensitively, 'What are we going to do about her money?' That was another remark he regrets. 'I've never forgiven myself for that,' he says. 'Really, deep down, you know, I never have quite forgiven myself for that. But that's all I could say then.' And when Lennon died, all he could say was, 'It's a drag.'

He sat at home that night, watching the news on television, holding hands with his wife and children and crying. 'We just couldn't handle it, really,' he said.

And what hurt most of all, in those desperate days after Lennon's death when the enormity of the loss was still sinking in, was, McCartney said, that 'we never actually sat down and straightened our differences out'. A decade and a host of debilitating lawsuits later, Lennon and McCartney were still at war over the spoils of the Beatle's fortune. It was a feud that had carried through till death finally parted them. It would continue beyond the grave.

Mae C Jemison
Toyomi Igus

Though less well known that Yuri Gagarin or Neil Armstrong, Mae C Jemison deserves a place in the history of space travel as the first black female astronaut. This entry is from a book which features many successful black women in different fields of human endeavour.

First Black Female Astronaut
1956–
Birthplace: Decatur, Alabama

The most important challenge in my life is to always test the limits of my abilities, do the best job I can at the time while remaining true to myself.

In August 1987, Dr. Mae Jemison was sitting at her desk at a hospital in Los Angeles. She was between patients, taking care of some paperwork, when the phone rang. It was a representative of the National Aeronautics and Space Administration (NASA). The young physician was told she had been chosen as an astronaut candidate. She could become the first African-American woman to travel in space.

This was just the latest in a series of notable accomplishments by the multitalented Mae Jemison. Born in Alabama but raised in Chicago, Mae received her bachelor of science degree in chemical engineering and a bachelor of arts degree in African and Afro-American Studies simultaneously at Stanford University. From there she enrolled in Cornell University Medical College where she became very active in student and community-based groups. She also maintained her interest in Third World countries. Mae travelled to Cuba, Kenya, and Thailand to work and continue her medical training.

After graduating from medical school, Mae joined the Peace Corps and worked in Africa supervising health-care programs for Peace Corps personnel. Upon her return, she worked as a general practitioner in Los Angeles. She then applied for admission to the astronaut program.

Three months after Mae first applied to NASA, the *Challenger* disaster occurred, taking the lives of seven astronauts, including that of an African American, Ronald McNair. But the incident did not deter Mae. She simply reapplied when the selection process was reopened. A year later, she was notified that she had been chosen from nearly 2,000 applicants as one of the 15 members of NASA's 1987 astronaut-training program.

Mae C Jemison travelled into space in August 1992 on Space Lab J, a joint venture between the United States and Japan focusing on life sciences.

Marilyn Monroe

Marilyn Monroe was one of the most famous film stars of the twentieth century, remembered in different ways by different people. She was a talented and beautiful actress; and this is how people remember her. But others recall that her success and celebrity lifestyle could not prevent her from becoming lonely and depressed.

Here are two encyclopedia entries on her. The first is from Encarta which is available only on CD-ROM; the second is from an encyclopedia aimed at younger readers, aged about 11 to 14.

Monroe, Marilyn (1926-1962), American motion-picture actor, who became the most famous international sex symbol of the 20th century. Born Norma Jean Mortenson in Los Angeles, the daughter of an emotionally unstable mother, she spent a troubled childhood in foster homes and orphanages and at the age of 16 entered into an ill-fated marriage. In 1944, while working in a defense plant, she was noticed by a United State Army photographer who induced her to pose for posters for the troops. Instantly popular as a model, Monroe soon found other assignments and registered with a modeling agency, which sent her to charm school and put her on a number of magazine covers. She was signed by Fox Film Corporation in 1946 but had only two small film roles before she was dropped by the studio. In 1948 she was briefly under contract to Columbia Pictures, and although she was soon out of work again, this stint yielded appearances in a low-budget musical, *Ladies of the Chorus* (1949), and in the film *Love Happy* (1949), in which she had a bit part with the Marx Brothers.

In 1950 Fox studios signed Monroe to another contract, and over the next few years she appeared in a series of small parts in films that began to gain her increased attention. Notable among these were *Asphalt Jungle* (1950) and *All About Eve* (1950). Monroe also appeared in *Love Nest* (1951), *Clash by Night* (1952), and *Monkey Business* (1952; with Cary Grant and Ginger Rogers) and had her first lead role in *Don't Bother to Knock* (1952), as a psychotic babysitter. By 1953 she was appearing as a star in such films as *Niagara, How to Marry a Millionaire,* and *Gentlemen Prefer Blondes* (as Lorelei Lee).

The sex-symbol phase of her career followed, in which her wide-eyed charm, physical voluptuousness, and natural sex appeal made her internationally renowned and her looks and mannerisms were widely imitated. Famous films of this period, during which she was Fox's leading box-office attraction, include *River of No Return* (1954), *There's No Business Like Show Business* (1954), and *The Seven-Year Itch* (1955; directed by Billy Wilder). In 1954 Monroe married baseball player Joe DiMaggio, but they were divorced a year later. In 1955 she rebelled against her long succession of stereotyped roles, announced that she was forming her own production company, and went to New York City to attend classes at the Actors Studio. She was, however, subsequently induced to remain at Fox with a contract that offered her more creative control. In 1956 she married playwright Arthur Miller, whom she had met in New York City and who later scripted her last film. She made *The Prince and the Showgirl* – a critical and commercial failure – with Laurence Olivier in 1957, gave a noted performance as the singer Sugar Kane in *Some Like it Hot* (1959; directed by Wilder), and appeared with Yves Montand in *Let's Make Love* (1960).

During this period, under the constant care of a psychiatrist, beset by depression and illness, and prone to mix prescription drugs with alcohol, Monroe was becoming increasingly unreliable. Her final film was *The Misfits* (1961), written for her by Miller and directed by John Huston. A week after the film opened, she divorced Miller. In the summer of 1962 she was fired from the set of her latest picture, and a month later she was found dead in her home, the apparent victim of a barbiturate overdose (although suicide was not ruled out).

Monroe's autobiography, *My Story*, appeared in 1974, and many celebrity biographies and collections of still photographs of her have also been published. In addition, her life has been the subject of several documentaries and fictionalized film treatments.

Monroe, Marilyn
1926–1962

Marilyn's real name was Norma Jean Baker or Mortenson. She had a miserable childhood in Los Angeles foster homes because her mother was mentally ill. Even when she later became a famous actress, she could still feel lonely and unloved at times.

After working as a model and in minor film roles, she found her first big role in *Niagara* in 1953. Two of her best known films, *Gentlemen Prefer Blondes* (1953) and *Some Like It Hot* (1959), show she was a fine comic actress. However, she also took serious, dramatic roles in films like *Bus Stop* (1956) and *The Misfits* (1961), her last film.

She had several husbands, including baseball star Joe DiMaggio and playwright Arthur Miller. She died from a drug overdose in 1962. Even now, many years after her death, she is remembered as one of the most beautiful stars of cinema history.

Charles Dickens
Peter Ackroyd

Charles Dickens has become one of the most popular of all writers. Characters he created, such as the villainous Fagin, or the mean Mr Scrooge, are famous the world over. He based many of his stories on things that had happened to him as a child. In this extract his biographer, Peter Ackroyd (himself a novelist, like Dickens), describes moments from Dickens's harsh childhood, when he had to work all day packaging bottles of shoe-blacking.

When Dickens first came to Bayham Street, the 'night-life' of London fascinated him; particularly he was struck by the world of Seven Dials – '. . . what wild visions of prodigies of wickedness, want, and beggary, arise in my mind out of that place!' But now there came a time when that life would come all too close to him. It began with James Lamert. He was no longer living with the Dickens family – no doubt the want of space and the noise of small children had something to do with his decision – but he had been approached by his cousin, George Lamert, to become the chief manager of a business he had just purchased. This was Warren's Blacking of 30 Hungerford Stairs, a manufacturer of boot blacking, and it was James Lamert's suggestion that Charles, now entering his twelfth year, should also be employed there at a salary of six or seven shillings a week. Dickens himself put the matter baldly: '. . . the offer was accepted very willingly by my father and mother, and on a Monday morning I went down to the blacking warehouse to begin my business life.' The date generally fixed for this inauspicious occasion is Monday, 9 February, 1824, just two days after his twelfth birthday. It might have seemed to him '. . . some dark conspiracy to thrust him forth upon the world', to use the words in *Oliver Twist*, but to his parents it must have been a welcome opportunity for their son to be gainfully employed and to help with their own **straitened** finances. In a business run by their kind relative, after all, what rungs might their son not climb on the journey towards gentility?

And so on that fateful Monday he walked the three miles from Camden Town to the Strand, down Hampstead Road and Tottenham Court Road, crossing the High Street which leads into Broad St Giles's and then down St Martin's Lane. Then across the Strand into an area of squalid corners and alleys, and descending Hungerford Stairs to the river itself. His destination was the last house on the left, beside the Thames itself, '. . . a crazy, tumbledown old house, abutting of course on the river, and literally overrun with rats. Its **wainscotted** rooms and its rotten floors and staircase, and the old grey rats swarming down in the cellars, and the sound of their squeaking and scuffling coming up the stairs at all times, and the dirt and decay of the place, rise up visibly before me, as if I were there again.'

This was the place to which the twelve-year-old Dickens came, then. James Lamert greeted him, and took him to the counting house on the first floor; there was an alcove there, looking down at the Thames, which was to be his place of work. A boy who worked downstairs, Bob Fagin, was called up to show Dickens of what that work would consist: he was to take the bottles of blacking and prepare them for sale. Not bottles exactly, but receptacles rather like small flower pots made of earthenware and with a rim

straitened: tight, suffering from difficulties
wainscotted: with a wooden panel running round the lower half of the walls

around them for string. Dickens's job was '. . . to cover
the pots of paste-blacking: first with a piece of oil-paper,
and then with a piece of blue paper; to tie them round
with a string; and then to clip the paper close and neat all
round.' When he had finished a few gross of these, 'I was
to paste on each a printed label'. He worked for ten hours
a day, with a meal break at twelve and a tea-break in the
late afternoon. The boy himself, '. . . of singular abilities:
quick, eager, delicate, and soon hurt, bodily or mentally',
now sitting at a work-table with scissors and string and
paste, looking out at the dreary river just beneath him,
bearing away his hopes. It is not too much to say that his
childhood came suddenly to an end, together with that
world of reading and imagination in which the years of his
childhood had been passed. But it was not gone; it had
ended so suddenly that it did not gradually fade and
disappear as most childhoods do. Instead it was preserved
in the amber of Dickens's rich memory. 'My whole nature
was so penetrated with the grief and humiliation of such
considerations, and even now, famous and caressed and
happy, I often forget in my dreams that I have a dear wife
and children; even that I am a man; and wander desolately
back to that time of my life.'

ACTIVITIES

David Beckham

1 Write notes of the sequence of events leading up to Beckham's sending-off and what happened after it, to create a clear picture of what took place. For example:

> 1   The second half begins.
> 2   Simeone crashes into Beckham.

2 This extract was written by a journalist, Mark Palmer. Imagine that you are the radio commentator for the match. Use Mark Palmer's account to write your commentary for **a)** the moments surrounding Beckham's sending-off and **b)** the penalty shoot-out. Then perform it as dramatically as you can. You could begin at the point just before Simeone's tackle:

> Beckham collects the ball on the right just inside the Argentina half . . .

3 How can you tell that this account was written by an England supporter? Pick out all the phrases which show that the writer is biased in favour of England. You might start your list with:

> - 'Simeone patted him on the head for the benefit of the referee . . . ' (page 3)
> - 'the Argentinian captain went down clutching at various parts of his leg as if amputation was imminent . . .' (page 3)

Rewrite the opening section of the account as though you were an Argentinian journalist. Then discuss all the differences with a partner.

Ewan McGregor

1 The *Star Wars* films have clearly played an important part in Ewan McGregor's life so far.

- What was the name of his uncle, who was in the film?
- What part did he play? What did his character do in the film? What line did he say?
- The uncle lived in London. Why did he stand out as being different when he visited them in Perthshire?
- How old was Ewan when he saw the first *Star Wars* film?
- What would Ewan have enjoyed?
- How did the film affect Ewan's brother Colin?

2 The person a biographer writes about is called the 'subject'. Many biographers like to find things which happened in their subject's childhood which help to explain the way they grow up. In this biography, Uncle Denis is named as an important influence in his nephew's choice of future career.

Write down the facts we are told about Uncle Denis in the extract. Then, next to each fact, say what influence you think it might have had upon young Ewan McGregor. You might draw up two columns, like this:

Facts about Uncle Denis (things known to be true)	Uncle Denis's influence on Ewan McGregor
• He had long hair and dressed strangely	Ewan found him exciting
• He acted in the Perth Theatre pantomime	
• He played . . .	

Claire Danes and Leonardo DiCaprio

Use the information in the extract to write a 'question and answer' article for a magazine. Put a series of questions to the director, Baz Luhrmann, about Claire Danes, Leonardo DiCaprio and their work on *Romeo + Juliet*. For example, the article might begin with a short introduction about the film, the director and its stars, followed by questions, like this:

Film: *Romeo + Juliet*
Director: . . .
Stars: . . .

Q: You had difficulty in finding a Juliet. What made you pick Claire Danes?
Luhrmann: *In the audition she was the only one who . . .*
Q: What did DiCaprio say about Claire Danes's audition?
L: *He said that . . .*
Q: What did you know about Claire Danes at that time?
L: . . .
Q: How did DiCaprio and Danes get on during the early days of filming?
L: . . .
Q: Did they ever argue?
L: . . .
Q: Did you have any concerns about the way the actors would handle Shakespeare's language?
L: . . .
Q: What did you do in rehearsals to help make the language clear?
L: . . .
Q: Did DiCaprio find it easy playing Romeo?
L:

Paul McCartney

1 This extract is taken from a book about Paul McCartney. In it, the biographer (Ross Benson) records how McCartney regretted saying to a reporter 'It's a drag', when told of John Lennon's murder.

Imagine that you are the reporter McCartney spoke to, and write **a)** the headline and **b)** the (brief) article which your newspaper will publish. You will need to think about:

a) the headline
   - What main point do you want to make in the headline?
   - How will you grab the reader's attention?
b) the article
   - How will you set the scene?
   - What do you want to say about McCartney's comment on Lennon's death?

2 Now write a more sympathetic article, by a different reporter who has had a chance to talk to McCartney about his feelings. The second reporter might choose to include McCartney's own words, such as:

- 'It was all blurred . . . You couldn't take it in.' (page 15)
- 'I meant drag in the heaviest sense of the word' (page 16)
- 'I've never forgiven myself for that' (page 16)
- 'We just couldn't handle it, really.' (page 16)

Mae C Jemison

This article is from a book which contains a series of short biographies, all written very plainly and with an emphasis on facts, rather than opinions or emotions.

1 Which facts might go on Mae C Jemison's CV if she were applying for a job? Copy and complete the following form:

Name:	Mae Jemison
Date and place of birth:	
Where were you brought up?	
Which university/universities did you attend?	
Degree subjects (i) (ii) (iii)	
Activities as a student:	
Interests:	
Travel:	
Employment after graduation:	

2 Imagine that you are Mae C Jemison and have been asked by a magazine to write your own account of the time between the phone call from NASA and the end of your training as an astronaut. Draft a brief opening to your article, using the facts given here, but adding some comments about your feelings and responses.

You could begin:

> I can remember it very clearly. I was sitting at my desk in the Los Angeles hospital where I was working. It was around the middle of August in 1987.

You could include answers to the following questions:
- What were you doing when the phone rang?
- Who was the phone call from, and what did they say?
- How did you feel?

Marilyn Monroe

1 Make a list of the main facts in the Encarta entry and then do the same for the shorter article.

Which facts have been omitted from the encyclopedia aimed at younger readers? Pick three and say why you think they might have been left out. For example, your list might start off like this:

Encarta	Children's encyclopedia
• American motion-picture actor • international sex-symbol • born: Norma Jean Mortenson •	• film roles • – • real name . . .

2 Look at the accounts of Marilyn Monroe's death, and make a list of the facts given. You will see that there are some differences: in pairs, discuss why the two writers might have chosen to include different facts. What other differences are there in the facts given?

3 One of these entries is aimed at adults, the other at children. The writers have therefore had to make choices about the kind of language they use. Find examples of the differences in:
- sentence length
- simple and complex sentences
- vocabulary.

Charles Dickens

When he was planning to write a biography of Dickens, Peter Ackroyd decided to use quotations from Dickens's own novels to describe moments in the novelist's life. You can identify them easily in the extract because they are in quotation marks. A number of them are taken from *David Copperfield* and *Oliver Twist*, for example.

Here are the opening words of some of the quotations you could choose from:
- 'what wild visions . . .' (page 22)
- 'the offer was accepted very willingly by my father and mother . . .' (page 22)
- 'some dark conspiracy . . .' (page 23)
- 'a crazy, tumbledown old house . . .' (page 23)
- 'to cover the pots of paste-blacking . . .' (page 23)
- 'of singular abilities . . .' (page 24)
- 'my whole nature . . .' (page 24)

There are several more in the extract. Pick three or four which you find particularly vivid. What do you think they add to the story of Dickens's childhood as Ackroyd tells it? Can you say why they are so effective?

Comparing the extracts

1 Which of the biographies in this section did you find most interesting? In small groups, talk about:

a) which extracts made you interested in the subject, and why;

b) which extracts told you something which you didn't know before;

c) which extracts made you interested in someone you hadn't really thought much about before.

Now, on your own, make a list of what in your opinion makes a good biography.

2 Write a section from a biography of your own. Before you start, look back at the extracts in this section to give you some ideas. You could choose to

- write about the first person to do something (Mae C Jemison)
- defend someone's actions (as Mark Palmer does for David Beckham)
- show how something in childhood had a lasting effect (Ewan McGregor)
- describe an important meeting (Claire Danes and Leonardo DiCaprio)
- explain a mistake that the person later regretted (Paul McCartney)

When you are ready to begin, follow this step-by-step approach:

- First choose a subject – someone you are really interested in and know something about
- Next, decide what kind of biography you want to write (an encyclopedia article, such as one of the two examples on Marilyn Monroe; a section from a complete life story (such as the one on Dickens); an account of an important episode in the person's life (like the extract about Claire Danes and Leonardo DiCaprio)

- Consult books, magazines, the Internet – any other sources you can think of – to find out more about your chosen person
- Then jot down all the main details that you know about the person: where they were born, what they have done in their career, what their interests are . . .

If your biography is about a writer, an actor or singer, you could use quotations from their own work, as Peter Ackroyd does in his biography of Dickens. (A biography of Robbie Williams might contain lines from his songs, for example.)

To help you, here is a writing frame based on the children's encyclopedia entry on Marilyn Monroe.

MARILYN MONROE 1926-1962		
Paragraph	Topic	Introductory sentence
1	• her real name	*Marilyn's real name was . . .*
	• early life	*She had a miserable childhood . . .*
2	• early work and first film roles	*After working as a model . . .*
	• best-known films	*Two of her best-known films . . .*
	• serious roles	*However, she also took serious, dramatic roles . . .*
3	• her private life	*She had several husbands . . .*
	• her death	*She died from . . .*
	• how people remember her today	*Even now, many years after her death . . .*

Section 2
AUTOBIOGRAPHY

People decide to write their life stories for many different reasons. Some of the extracts in this section are by people who went through experiences which they knew to be of historical importance. Mary Seacole, for example, had been a nurse in the Crimean War of the 1850s and had seen the suffering of the soldiers at first hand; Emmeline Pankhurst was one of the first people to fight for women's right to vote, at the beginning of the twentieth century.

Other writers simply want to say something about the funny or unusual things that have happened to them. Gerald Durrell recalls a time when he narrowly escaped being eaten by piranhas, while Bill Bryson has a nasty encounter with a fridge full of junk food!

Tom Baker

These days we are used to amazing special effects in science fiction films. This extract was written in 1997 and describes how, when the actor Tom Baker played Doctor Who in the 1970s, one of his most terrifying weapons was a bag of jelly babies . . .

When we were rehearsing at BBC North Acton, the chaps playing the Daleks never wore their top bits. This meant that during the scenes when they were threatening me,

they held out their right arms in place of the regular sink plungers. They took it all very seriously, of course, and this only added to the fun.

As the rehearsals went on it seemed to me that the BBC was missing an opportunity to make two programmes for the price of one. If they had recorded the rehearsals and the arguments that went on, they could have cut some excellent stuff for light entertainment. Our director, David Maloney, had just as much difficulty as the rest of us keeping a straight face. Michael Wisher, who can seriously be described as the creator of the character of Davros, used to work with a kilt on and a paper bag over his head to maintain his feel for the part*. He took his work so seriously that he would not remove the bag even at coffee break. To see coffee and biscuits being pushed under the paper bag, followed by a cigarette, while the bag continued to express the most passionate views on how Davros felt about things was just bliss. He did allow us to make a hole in the top of his bag so that the smoke could escape.

During the shooting of 'Planet of Evil' we filmed at Ealing Studios before going back to the BBC for the rehearsals of the interior shots at North Acton. Philip Hinchcliffe [the director] was not at the last day of filming and his absence led to a happy coincidence. There was a scene in which I had to seize some poor alien and threaten to kill him with a knife in order to persuade his comrades to reveal their leader to me. It was a very ordinary little scene; so ordinary that I hadn't really read it properly. When the knife was offered to me I felt suddenly impatient and then disgusted with the idea of using such a coarse threat in our lovely programme. The line I was to say ran, 'Take me to your leader or I'll kill him

---

* Davros, for those who don't remember, wore an ugly mask (which Michael couldn't see through) and had no legs.

with this knife'. Yes, I think it was as plonking as that. So I refused to say it. We had very little time left on our final day of filming to get this scene in the can and my refusal caused a problem for David Maloney, the director. In Philip's absence he had to log the scene I was causing about my lines. I didn't really care. David and I were very friendly colleagues and he knew I was not just being difficult. But, without the producer there, who could take responsibility for a line change? Me, of course.

We rolled the cameras and, as written, I grabbed some pitiful little native of Zeta Minor, pulled him close, and said: 'Take me to your leader or I'll kill him with this deadly jelly baby'. When the other little Zetas agreed to comply, I bit the head off the jelly baby (orange was my favourite) and I think I offered the rest of it to the captured Zeta. That's the way I remember it. I don't think David Maloney was too thrilled with my effort and, reading this now, neither am I, but there you are, we did, and that was the end of filming. We all went off to resume our lives and met up again a few days later at North Acton for the rehearsals. I asked David how the **rushes** were and he said they were fine (directors and producers always say that rushes are fine, sometimes they say they are fantastic and sometimes some actors believe them). But a few minutes after I had seen David in came Philip Hinchcliffe.

'How were the rushes?' I asked him.

'Oh, terrific,' said Philip, 'really fantastic. I loved that bit with the jelly baby.'

When the last episode was aired, the children loved the scene and realised that I was bluffing the Zetas who wouldn't know a jelly baby from a kangaroo. It made just as much or little sense as a knife.

rushes: sections of film shot that day

It was really gratifying to have had that little bit of encouragement from Philip, since most of my ideas were thrown out very quickly. I hold no grudges against anyone for that reaction because most of my ideas were truly terrible.

All this happened in October 1975. A few weeks ago, in a bookshop in Manchester, a child of about ten offered me a jelly baby. He was so happy when I laughed, then he quoted my line, and it was my turn to be happy.

Gerald Durrell

If you're a very strong swimmer, it isn't usually too scary trying to get across a lake. But when you're in South America, it's a good idea to listen to your guide when he advises you not to jump in. For Gerald Durrell and his friend Bob, things might have ended rather nastily . . .

Bob joined me, and we sat and stared at the flat, shining expanse of water.

'What about swimming across?' suggested Bob.

I measured the distance suspiciously with my eyes.

'It's about half a mile, I should say. I don't see why we shouldn't, if we take it easy.'

'Well, I'm willing to have a try. We've walked all this way to see the Amerindians, and I don't see why we should go back until we've seen them,' said Bob **pugnaciously**.

'All right,' I said, 'we'll have a shot at it.'

We removed our clothes and waded out naked into the lake.

'What you going to do, Chief?' said Cordai [their guide] in alarm.

'Swim across,' I said airily.

'But, Chief, it's not a good place to swim.'

'Why not?' I enquired coldly. 'You said that *you'd* swum across it many times.'

'It's too far for you, Chief,' said Cordai feebly.

'Nonsense, my good man. Why, this chief here has got several medals for swimming across lakes which in comparison to this would seem like the Atlantic.'

pugnaciously: aggressively

This successfully crushed Cordai, who was not at all sure what a medal was. We waded out, and by the time we had reached the edge of the reed-beds we were up to our necks in warm honey-coloured waters. We paused for a moment to survey the opposite bank and see which was the nearest point to head for, and I suddenly realised that neither Bob nor I had removed our hats. There was something so ludicrous about the sight of Bob splashing about in the dark waters, doggedly doing the breast-stroke, with an elegant green pork-pie hat set at a jaunty angle over one eye, that I got an attack of the giggles.

'What's the matter?' asked Bob.

I trod water and gasped for breath.

'Intrepid Explorer Swims Lake In Hat,' I spluttered.

'You've got yours on too.'

'That's in case we meet any female Indians on the other side. Dammit, man, one must have a hat to raise to a lady. Where are your gentlemanly instincts?'

Elaborating this theme we became quite weak with laughter. We were floating on our backs to recover, when we heard a series of plops, and the water ahead of us was rippled by something beneath the surface. From the bank we heard Ivan and Cordai shouting:

'Come back, Chief, they bad fish,' came Cordai's voice. 'I think they're piranhas, sir,' came Ivan's cultured accents.

Bob and I glanced at each other, and at the ripples which were rapidly approaching, and then we both turned and swam back to shore at a speed that would certainly have won us a couple of medals in any swimming-pool. We emerged dripping and gasping but still wearing our ridiculous headgear.

'Were they piranhas?' I asked Ivan, as soon as I had recovered my breath.

'I don't know, sir,' he replied, 'but it would not be safe to risk it in case they *are*.'

'I couldn't agree with you more,' panted Bob.

It may be necessary to explain that the piranha is one of the most unpleasant freshwater fish known. It is a flat, corpulent, silver-coloured fish, with the lower jaw protruded, so that in profile it looks exactly like a bulldog. This mouth is armed with one of the most fearsome sets of teeth to be found in the fish world. They are triangular in shape and so arranged that when the fish closes its mouth they interlock with the precision of a cog-wheel. Piranhas live in schools in most of the tropical South American rivers, and they have earned for themselves a vivid reputation. They appear to have an ability to smell blood underwater for considerable distances, and at the first whiff of it, they all congregate with incredible speed at the spot and with their dreadful teeth proceed to tear the object to pieces. The thoroughness with which they can dismantle a living or dead body is illustrated by an experiment that was once carried out. A capybara, a large South American rodent that grows to the size of a big dog, was killed, and its corpse was hung in a river infested by piranhas. The capybara weighed a hundred pounds, but its fat body had been stripped to a skeleton within *fifty-five seconds*. On examination of the skeleton it was found that some of the fish had bitten clean through the ribs in their frenzied efforts to tear off the flesh. Whether or not the fish in the lake had been piranhas I don't know, but I think we did the wisest thing in coming out, for you can't go swimming among hungry piranhas and live to profit by your mistake.

Clive James

We have become used to all sorts of luxuries in the modern world. In this extract Clive James, the popular broadcaster and journalist, remembers his childhood in Australia in the 1940s, before the days when houses had flushing toilets. Lavatories were down the garden and their waste had to be collected each week by the dunny man . . .

Ever since I could remember, the dunny man had come running down the driveway once a week. From inside the house, we could hear his running footsteps. Then we could hear the rattle and thump as he lifted the lavatory, took out the full pan, clipped on a special lid, and set down an empty pan in its place. After more rattling and banging, there was an audible intake of breath as he hefted the full pan on to his shoulder. Then the footsteps went back along the driveway, slower this time but still running. From outside in the street there was rattling, banging and shouting as the full pan was loaded on to the dunny cart along with all the other full pans. I often watched the dunny cart from the front window. As it slowly made its noisome way down the street, the dunny men ran to and from it with awesome expertise. They wore shorts, sand-shoes, and nothing else except a sun-tan suspiciously deep on the forearms. Such occasional glimpses were all one was allowed by one's parents and all that was encouraged even by the dunny men themselves. They preferred to work in nobody's company except their own. They were a band apart.

Years went by without those running footsteps being acknowledged by any other means except a bottle of beer left standing in the lavatory on the closest visiting day to Christmas Day. Otherwise it seemed generally agreed that the lavatory pan was changed by magic. From day to day it got fuller and fuller, generating maggots by about the third day. To combat the smell, honeysuckle was grown on a trellis outside the lavatory door, in the same way that the European nobility had recourse to perfume when they travelled by galley. The maggots came from blowflies and more blowflies came from the maggots. Blowflies were called blowies. The Australian climate, especially on the Eastern seaboard in the latitude of Sydney, was specifically designed to accommodate them. The blowies' idea of a good time was to hang around the dunny waiting for the seat to be lifted. They were then faced with the challenge of getting through the hole before it was blocked by the descending behind of the prospective occupant. There was no time for any fancy flying. Whether parked on the wall or stacking around in a holding pattern near the ceiling, every blowie was geared up to make either a vertical dive from high altitude or a death-defying low-level run through the rapidly decreasing airspace between the seat and your descending arse. The moment the seat came up, suddenly it was **Pearl Harbour**.

Once inside, enclosed under a dark sky, the blowies set about dumping their eggs. God knows what would have happened if ever the dunny men had gone on strike. Even as things were, by the end of the week the contents of the pan would be getting too close for comfort. Luckily the dunny man was a model of **probity**. Never putting a foot wrong, he carried out his **Sisyphean** task in loyal

---

Pearl Harbour: the place where the American fleet was destroyed by the Japanese airforce in 1941, bringing the United States into the Second World War
probity: honesty, upright behaviour
Sisyphean: in Greek mythology, Sisyphus was condemned to endlessly push a huge boulder uphill

silence. Only when he was about to leave our lives for ever did his concentration slip. Perhaps he foresaw that one day the sewer would come to everywhere in the world. Perhaps, in order to ward off these grim thoughts, he partook of his Christmas beer while still engaged in the task. Because it was on that day – the day before Christmas Eve – that the dunny man made his solitary mistake.

My mother and I were having breakfast. I heard the dunny man's footsteps thumping along the driveway, with a silent pause as he hurdled my bicycle, which in my habitual carelessness I had left lying there. I heard the usual thumps, bangs and heaves. I could picture the brimming pan, secured with the special clipped lid, hoisted high on his shoulder while he held my mother's gift bottle of beer in his other, appreciative hand. Then the footsteps started running back the other way. Whether he forgot about my bicycle, or simply mistimed his jump, there was no way of telling. Suddenly there was the noise of . . . well, it was mainly the noise of a dunny man running full tilt into a bicycle. The uproar was made especially ominous by the additional noise – tiny but significant in context – of a clipped lid springing off.

While my mother sat there with her hands over her eyes I raced out through the fly-screen door and took a look down the driveway. The dunny man, overwhelmed by the magnitude of his tragedy, had not yet risen to his feet. Needless to say, the contents of the pan had been fully divulged. All the stuff had come out. But what was really remarkable was the way none of it had missed him. Already you could hear a **gravid** hum in the air. Millions of flies were on their way towards us. They were coming from all over Australia. For them, it was **a Durbar**, **a moot**, a gathering of the clans. For us, it was the end of an era.

gravid: heavy, as though full of something
a Durbar: great gathering of people called by an Indian prince
a moot: an important assembly in Anglo-Saxon times

Bill Bryson

Bill Bryson, an American writer, came to Britain in 1973 – and stayed for nearly twenty years. When he went back, he had to get used to all sorts of things, including the horrors of American junk food.

I decided to clean out the fridge the other day. We don't usually clean out our fridge – we just box it up every four or five years and send it off to the Centers for Disease Control in Atlanta with a note to help themselves to anything that looks scientifically promising – but we hadn't seen one of the cats for a few days and I had a vague recollection of having glimpsed something furry on the bottom shelf towards the back. (Turned out to be a large piece of Gorgonzola.)

So there I was, down on my knees unwrapping pieces of foil and peering cautiously into Tupperware containers, when I came across an interesting product called a breakfast pizza and I examined it with a kind of rueful fondness, as you might regard an old photograph of yourself dressed in clothes that you cannot believe you ever thought were stylish. The breakfast pizza, you see, represented the last surviving relic of a bout of very serious retail foolishness on my part.

Some weeks ago I announced to my wife that I was going to the supermarket with her next time she went because the stuff she kept bringing home was – how can I put this? – not fully in the spirit of American eating. Here we were living in a paradise of junk food – the country that gave the world cheese in a spray can – and she kept bringing home healthy stuff like fresh broccoli and packets of Ryvita.

It was because she was English, of course. She didn't really understand the rich, unrivalled possibilities for greasiness and goo that the American diet offers. I longed for artificial bacon bits, melted cheese in a shade of yellow unknown to nature, and creamy chocolate fillings, sometimes all in the same product. I wanted food that squirts when you bite into it or plops onto your shirt front in such gross quantities that you have to rise carefully from the table and limbo over to the sink to clean yourself up. So I accompanied her to the supermarket and while she was off squeezing melons and pricing mushrooms I made for the junk food section – which was essentially all the rest of the store. Well, it was heaven.

The breakfast cereals alone could have occupied me for most of the afternoon. There must have been 200 types, and I am not exaggerating. Every possible substance that could be dried, puffed and coated with sugar was there. The most immediately arresting was a cereal called Cookie Crisp, which tried to pretend it was a nutritious breakfast but was really just chocolate chip cookies that you put in a bowl and ate with milk. Brilliant.

Also of note were cereals called Peanut Butter Crunch, Cinnamon Mini Buns, Count Chocula ('with Monster Marshmallows'), and a particularly hardcore offering called Cookie Blast Oat Meal, which contained *four* kinds of cookies. I grabbed one of each of the cereals and two of the oatmeal – how often I've said that you shouldn't start a day without a big steaming bowl of cookies – and sprinted with them back to the trolley.

'What's that?' my wife asked in the special tone of voice with which she often addresses me in retail establishments.

I didn't have time to explain. 'Breakfast for the next six months,' I panted as I dashed past, 'and don't even *think* about putting any of it back and getting muesli.'

I had no idea how the market for junk food had proliferated. Everywhere I turned I was confronted with foods guaranteed to make you waddle, most of which were entirely new to me – jelly creme pies, moon pies, pecan spinwheels, peach mellos, root beer buttons, chocolate fudge devil dogs and a whipped marshmallow sandwich spread called Fluff, which came in a tub large enough to bath a baby in.

You really cannot believe the bounteous variety of non-nutritious foods available to the American supermarket shopper these days or the quantities in which they are consumed. I recently read that the average American eats 17.8 *pounds* of pretzels every year.

Aisle seven ('Food for the Seriously Obese') was especially productive. It had a whole section devoted exclusively to a product called Toaster Pastries, which included among much else, eight different types of toaster strudel. And what exactly is toaster strudel? Who cares? It was coated in sugar and looked drippy. I grabbed an armload.

I admit I got a little carried away – but there was so much and I had been away so long.

It was the breakfast pizza that finally made my wife snap. She looked at the box and said, 'No.'

'I beg your pardon, my sweet?'

'You are not bringing home something called breakfast pizza. I will let you have' – she reached into the trolley for some specimen samples – 'root beer buttons and toaster strudel and . . .' She lifted out a packet she hadn't noticed before. 'What's this?'

I looked over her shoulder. 'Microwave pancakes,' I said.

'Microwave pancakes,' she repeated, but with less enthusiasm.

'Isn't science wonderful?'

'You're going to eat it all,' she said. 'Every bit of everything that you don't put back on the shelves now. Do you understand that?'

'Of course,' I said in my sincerest voice.

And do you know she actually made me eat it. I spent weeks working my way through a symphony of American junk food, and it was all awful. Every bit of it. I don't know whether American junk food has got worse or whether my taste buds have matured, but even the treats I'd grown up with now seemed discouragingly pallid or disgustingly sickly.

The most awful of all was the breakfast pizza. I tried it three or four times, baked in the oven, zapped in the microwave, and once in desperation served it with a side of marshmallow Fluff, but it never rose beyond a kind of limp, chewy listlessness. Eventually I gave up altogether and hid the box in the Tupperware graveyard on the bottom shelf of the fridge.

Which is why, when I came across it again the other day, I regarded it with mixed feelings. I started to chuck it out, then hesitated and opened the lid. It didn't smell bad – I expect it was pumped so full of chemicals that there wasn't any room for bacteria – and I thought about keeping it a while longer as a reminder of my folly, but in the end I discarded it. And then, feeling peckish, I went off to the larder to see if I couldn't find a nice plain piece of Ryvita and maybe a stick of celery.

Laurie Lee

Laurie Lee's recollections about his childhood in the Gloucestershire countryside, *Cider with Rosie*, has become one of the most popular of all autobiographies. This account is of his first day at school in the early 1920s.

The village school at that time provided all the instruction we were likely to ask for. It was a small stone barn divided by a wooden partition into two rooms – The Infants and The Big Ones. There was one dame teacher, and perhaps a young girl assistant. Every child in the valley crowding there, remained till he was fourteen years old, then was presented to the working field or factory with nothing in his head more burdensome than a few **mnemonics**, a jumbled list of wars, and a dreamy image of the world's geography. It seemed enough to get by with, in any case; and was one up on our poor old grandparents.

This school, when I came to it, was at its peak. Universal education and **unusual fertility** had packed it to the walls with pupils. Wild boys and girls from miles around – from the outlying farms and half-hidden hovels way up at the ends of the valley – swept down each day to add to our numbers, bringing with them strange oaths and odours, quaint garments and curious pies. They were my first amazed vision of any world outside the womanly warmth of my family; I didn't expect to survive it for long, and I was confronted with it at the age of four.

mnemonics: phrases or patterns which help you remember something (e.g. 'spelling of necessary: one Collar, two Sleeves')
unusual fertility: more babies than usual had been born

The morning came, without any warning, when my sisters surrounded me, wrapped me in scarves, tied up my bootlaces, thrust a cap on my head, and stuffed a baked potato in my pocket.

'What's this?' I said.

'You're starting school today.'

'I ain't. I'm stopping 'ome.'

'Now, come on, Loll. You're a big boy now.'

'I ain't.'

'You are.'

'Boo-hoo.'

They picked me up bodily, kicking and bawling, and carried me up to the road.

'Boys who don't go to school get put in boxes, and turn into rabbits, and get chopped up Sundays.'

I felt this was overdoing it rather, but I said no more after that. I arrived at the school just three feet tall and fatly wrapped in my scarves. The playground roared like a rodeo, and the potato burned through my thigh. Old boots, ragged stockings, torn trousers and skirts, went skating and skidding around me. The rabble closed in; I was encircled; grit flew in my face like shrapnel. Tall girls with frizzled hair, and huge boys with sharp elbows, began to prod me with hideous interest. They plucked at my scarves, spun me round like a top, screwed my nose, and stole my potato.

I was rescued at last by a gracious lady – the sixteen-year-old junior-teacher – who boxed a few ears and dried my face and led me off to The Infants. I spent that first day picking holes in paper, then went home in a smouldering temper.

'What's the matter, Loll? Didn't he like it at school, then?'

'They never gave me the present!'

'Present? What present?'

'They said they'd give me a present.'

'Well, now, I'm sure they didn't.'

'They did! They said: "You're Laurie Lee, ain't you? Well, you just sit there for the present." I sat there all day but I never got it. I ain't going back there again!'

But after a week I felt like a veteran and grew as ruthless as anyone else. Somebody had stolen my baked potato, so I swiped somebody else's apple. The Infant Room was packed with toys such as I'd never seen before – coloured shapes and rolls of clay, stuffed birds and men to paint. Also a frame of counting beads which our young teacher played like a harp, leaning her bosom against our faces and guiding our wandering fingers.

My desk companions were those two blonde girls, already puppyishly pretty, whose names and bodies were to distract and haunt me for the next fifteen years of my life. Poppy and Jo were limpet chums; they sat holding hands all day; and there was a female self-possession about their pink sticky faces that made me shout angrily at them.

Vera was another I studied and liked; she was lonely, fuzzy, and short. I felt a curious compassion for stumpy Vera; and it was through her, and no beauty, that I got into trouble and received the first public shock of my life. How it happened was simple, and I was innocent, so it seemed. She came up to me in the playground one morning and held her face close to mine. I had a stick in my hand, so I hit her on the head with it. Her hair was springy, so I hit her again and watched her mouth open with a yell.

To my surprise a commotion broke out around me, cries of scandal from the older girls, exclamations of horror and heavy censure mixed with Vera's sobbing wails. I was intrigued, not alarmed, that by wielding a beech stick I was able to cause such a stir. So I hit her again, without spite or passion, then walked off to try something else.

The experiment might have ended there, and having ended would have been forgotten. But no; angry faces surrounded me, very red, all spitting and scolding.

'Horrid boy! Poor Vera! Little monster! Urgh! We're going to tell teacher about you!'

Something was wrong, the world seemed upset, I began to feel vaguely uneasy. I had only hit Vera on her wiry black hair, and now everybody was shouting at me. I ran and hid, feeling sure it would pass, but they hunted me down in the end. Two big righteous girls hauled me out by the ears.

'You're wanted in the Big Room, for 'itting Vera. You're 'alf going to cop it!' they said.

So I was dragged to that Room, where I'd never been before, and under the savage eyes of the elder children teacher gave me a scalding lecture. I was confused by now and shaking with guilt. At last I smirked and ran out of the room. I had learnt my first lesson, that I could not hit Vera, no matter how fuzzy her hair. And something else too; that the summons to the Big Room, the policeman's hand on the shoulder, comes almost always as a complete surprise, and for the crime that one has forgotten.

Emmeline Pankhurst

At the beginning of the twentieth century women did not have the vote in this country. Women who campaigned to get the vote at that period became known as suffragettes, and Emmeline Pankhurst was one of their foremost leaders. It was a difficult struggle. The suffragettes interrupted political meetings, smashed shop windows, chained themselves to railings and, when they were arrested, went on hunger strike, all in order to draw attention to their cause. In this extract from her autobiography, *My Own Story*, she describes the suffragettes' tactics to outwit the police and demonstrate for the cause of women's rights.

Whatever preparations the police department were making to prevent the demonstration, they failed because, while as usual, we were able to calculate exactly

53

what the police department were going to do, they were utterly unable to calculate what we were going to do. We had planned a demonstration for March 4th, and this one we announced. We planned another demonstration for March 1st, but this one we did not announce. Late in the afternoon of Friday, March 1st, I drove in a taxicab, accompanied by the Hon. Secretary of the Union, Mrs. Tuke and another of our members, to No. 10 Downing Street, the official residence of the Prime Minister. It was exactly half-past five when we alighted from the cab and threw our stones, four of them, through the window panes. As we expected we were promptly arrested and taken to Cannon Row police station. The hour that followed will long be remembered in London. At intervals of fifteen minutes relays of women who had volunteered for the demonstration did their work. The first smashing of glass occurred in the Haymarket and Piccadilly, and greatly startled and alarmed both pedestrians and police. A large number of the women were arrested, and everybody thought that this ended the affair. But before the excited **populace** and the frustrated shop owners' first exclamation had died down, before the police had reached the station with their prisoners, the ominous crashing and splintering of plate glass began again, this time along both sides of Regent Street and the Strand. A furious rush of police and people towards the second scene of action ensued. While their attention was being taken up with occurrences in this quarter, the third relay of women began breaking the windows in Oxford Circus and Bond Street. The demonstration ended for the day at half-past six with the breaking of many windows in the Strand. *Daily Mail* gave this graphic account of the demonstration:

populace: ordinary people

From every part of the crowded and brilliantly lighted streets came the crash of splintered glass. People started as windows shattered at their side; suddenly there was another crash in front of them; on the other side of the street; behind – everywhere. Scared shop assistants came running out to the pavements; traffic stopped; policemen sprang this way and that; five minutes later the streets were a procession of excited groups, each surrounding a woman wrecker being led in custody to the nearest police station. Meanwhile the shopping quarter of London had plunged itself into a sudden twilight. Shutters were hurriedly fitted, the rattle of iron curtains being drawn came from every side. Guards of commissionaires and shopmen were quickly mounted, and any unaccompanied lady in sight, especially, if she carried a hand bag, became an object of menacing suspicion.

At the hour when this demonstration was being made a conference was being held at Scotland Yard to determine what should be done to prevent the smashing of windows on the coming Monday night. But we had not announced the hour of our March 4th protest. I had in my speech simply invited women to assemble in Parliament Square on the evening of March 4th, and they accepted the invitation.

The demonstration had taken place in the morning, when a hundred or more women walked quietly into Knightsbridge and walking singly along the streets demolished nearly every pane of glass they passed. Taken by surprise the police arrested as many as they could reach, but most of the women escaped.

For that two days' work something like two hundred suffragettes were taken to the various police stations, and for days the long procession of women streamed through the courts. The dismayed magistrates found themselves facing, not only former rebels, but many new ones, in some cases, women whose names, like that of Dr. Ethel Smyth, the composer, were famous throughout Europe. These women, when **arraigned**, made clear and lucid statements of their positions and their motives, but magistrates are not schooled to examine motives. They are trained to think only of laws and mostly of laws protecting property. Their ears are not tuned to listen to words like those spoken by one of the prisoners, who said: 'We have tried every means – processions and meetings – which were of no avail. We have tried demonstrations, and now at last we have to break windows. I wish I had broken more. I am not in the least repentant. Our women are working in far worse conditions than the striking miners. I have seen widows struggling to bring up their children. Only two out of every five are fit to be soldiers. What is the good of a country like ours? England is absolutely on the wane. You only have one point of view, and that is the men's, and while men have done the best they could, they cannot go far without the women and the women's views. We believe the whole is in a muddle too horrible to think of.'

In 1918 women over the age of thirty were given the vote. All women were given the same voting rights as men in 1928, a month after Emmeline Pankhurst's death.

---

arraigned: brought to trial

Mary Seacole

Everybody has heard of Florence Nightingale and her nursing work in the Crimean War of the 1850s (in which Britain and her allies fought Russia). But Mary Seacole, who worked alongside her, having travelled the world as a doctor, is relatively unknown. Perhaps this is because she was black and the history books of the time did not consider her important enough to mention.

When the British government refused to pay Mary Seacole's expenses to travel to the Crimea, she used her own money and became a greatly loved and respected figure on the battlefield. This extract comes from her account of her experiences, *The Wonderful Adventures of Mrs Seacole in Many Lands*.

I saw the Russians cross and recross the river. I saw their officers cheer and wave them on in the coolest, bravest manner, until they were shot down by scores. I was near enough to hear at times, in the lull of artillery, and above the rattle of the musketry, the excited cheers which told of a daring attack or a successful repulse; and beneath where I stood I could see – what the Russians could not – steadily drawn up, quiet and expectant, the squadrons of English and French cavalry, calmly yet impatiently waiting until the Russians' partial success should bring their sabres into play. But the contingency never happened, and we saw the Russians fall slowly back in good order, while the dark-plumed Sardinians and red-pantalooned French spread out in pursuit, and formed a picture so excitingly beautiful that we forgot the suffering and death they left behind. And then I descended with the rest into the field of battle.

It was a fearful scene; but why repeat this remark. All death is **trying to witness** – even that of the good man who lays down his life hopefully and peacefully; but on the battle-field, where the poor body is torn and rent in hideous ways, and the scared spirit struggles to loose itself from the still strong frame that holds it tightly to the last, death is fearful indeed. It had come peacefully enough to some. They lay with half-opened eyes, and a quiet smile about the lips that showed their end to have been painless; others it had arrested in the heat of passion, and frozen on their pallid faces a glare of hatred and defiance that made your warm blood run cold. But little time had we to think of the dead, whose business it was to see after the dying, who might yet be saved. The ground was thickly **cumbered** with the wounded, some of them calm and resigned, others impatient and restless, a few filling the air with their cries of pain – all wanting water – and grateful to those who administered it, and more substantial comforts. You might see officers and strangers, visitors to the camp, riding about the field on this errand of mercy. And this, although – surely it could not have been intentional – Russian guns still played upon the scene of action. There were many others there, bent on a more selfish task. The plunderers were busy everywhere. It was marvellous to see how eagerly the French stripped the dead of what was valuable, not always, in their brutal work, paying much regard to the presence of a lady.

I attended to the wounds of many French and Sardinians, and helped to lift them into the ambulances which came tearing up to the scene of action. I derived no little gratification from being able to dress the wounds of several Russians; indeed, they were as kindly treated as

trying to witness: hard to watch
cumbered: covered, obstructed

the others. One of them was badly shot in the lower jaw, and was beyond my or any human skill. Incautiously I inserted my finger into his mouth to feel where the ball had lodged, and his teeth closed upon it, in the agonies of death, so tightly that I had to call to those around to release it, which was not done until it had been bitten so deeply that I shall carry the scar with me to my grave. Poor fellow, he meant me no harm, for, as the near approach of death softened his features, a smile spread over his rough inexpressive face, and so he died.

I attended another Russian, a handsome fellow, and an officer, shot in the side, who bore his cruel suffering with a firmness that was very noble. In return for the little use I was to him, he took a ring off his finger and gave it to me, and after I had helped to lift him into the ambulance he kissed my hand and smiled far more thanks than I had earned. I do not know whether he survived his wounds, but I fear not. Many others, on that day, gave me thanks in words the meaning of which was lost upon me, and all of them in that one common language of the whole world – smiles.

I carried two patients off the field; one a French officer wounded on the hip, who chose to go back to Spring Hill and be attended by me there, and who, on leaving, told us that he was a relative of the Marshal (Pelisser) [commander of the allied French army]; the other, a poor Cossack colt I found running round its dam, which lay beside its Cossack master dead, with its tongue hanging from its mouth. The colt was already wounded in the ears and fore-foot, and I was only just in time to prevent a French corporal who, perhaps for pity's sake, was preparing to give it its **coup de grâce**. I saved the poor

coup de grâce: here, the blow which would put the wounded animal out of its misery

thing by promising to give the Frenchman ten shillings if he would bring it down to the British Hotel, which he did that same evening. I attended to its hurts, and succeeded in rearing it, and it became a great pet at Spring Hill, and accompanied me to England.

I picked up some trophies from the battle-field, but not many, and those of little value. I cannot bear the idea of plundering either the living or the dead; but I picked up a Russian metal cross, and took from the bodies of some of the poor fellows nothing of more value than a few buttons, which I severed from their coarse grey coats.

So end my reminiscences of the battle of the Tchernaya, fought, as all the world knows, on the 16th August, 1855.

A year after the battle of the Tchernaya, the Crimean War ended. When Mary Seacole returned to England she had very little money left, but the soldiers did not forget her, and collected enough to keep her from poverty.

ACTIVITIES

Tom Baker

1 Daleks are among the most famous aliens in television science fiction. To appreciate Tom Baker's reminiscences, it helps to know something about them. In small groups, talk together to make sure that you know what they looked like and how they behaved. Do you know their one-word catch-phrase?

2 **a)** Write an article for a television magazine (such as the *Radio Times*) on Tom Baker and *Doctor Who*. Include some quotations from Tom Baker himself, such as:

- 'this only added to the fun' (page 35)
- 'who could take responsibility for a line change? Me, of course' (page 37)
- 'most of my ideas were truly terrible' (page 38)
- 'and it was my turn to be happy' (page 38).

b) Use a word-processor to design the page as it might look in the magazine. You could add illustrations of some of the moments that Tom Baker enjoyed most, such as:

- the actors rehearsing as Daleks
- Davros in the canteen with a paper bag over his head
- The Doctor threatening an alien with a jelly baby.

Gerald Durrell

1 Use the facts in the extract to draw up a 'Did you know' encyclopedia entry about the piranha. You could use the framework below:

The piranha

Its reputation:

- appearance _____

- teeth: _____

    their shape: _____

    their action: _____

- habitat: _____

- sense of smell: _____

- method of attack: _____

- experiment to show effects of attack by piranhas:

2 Gerald Durrell and his friend Bob ignore their guide Cordai's advice when they decide to swim across the lake. Write an account of the episode from Cordai's point of view. You might begin with:

> When Bob suggested swimming across, and Mr Durrell agreed, I tried to tell them that it wasn't a good idea. But they simply wouldn't listen to me . . .

Clive James

1 Clive James's memories are based around himself and the dunny man. But some of the funniest writing is his description of the flies, or 'blowies', when he compares them with aircraft or people rushing to a celebration. In pairs, talk about these comparisons and complete the grid below. For each example, decide

a) what Clive James is comparing the blowies with; and

b) whether you think it is an appropriate and funny comparison. The first example has been filled in to start you off:

Description	What are the blowies compared with?	Is the comparison appropriate and funny?
stacking around in a holding pattern	aircraft circling an airport waiting for permission to land	Yes. It is appropriate because you can imagine the flies up on the ceiling. It is funny to think of flies hanging around on a lavatory ceiling like highly organised airline pilots.
'geared up to make . . . a death-defying low-level run'		
'suddenly it was Pearl Harbour'		
'it was a Durbar, a moot, a gathering of the clans'		

2 Write up the incident of the dunny man as though it were a report in the local newspaper or on local radio. Remember that you have to choose language which will not offend readers or listeners.

First think up a witty, eye-catching headline.

Then decide on the main points to go in the article. You could mention:

- what the dunny man's usual arrangements were
- what happened on that particular morning (the bicycle . . . the beer . . . the crash . . . the end result!)

To help you, here is a writing frame for a tabloid newspaper article:

HEADLINE:	
Paragraph	Contents of the paragraph
1 (intro)	Set the scene: where did it happen; who was involved?
	What usually happened when the dunny man came?
2	What happened on that particular morning?
3	Quotations from (i) Mrs James and the young Clive, (ii) a neighbour; (iii) the dunny man himself.
4	Raise some questions (Does this mean the end of the dunny man era? Will the town now get mains drainage?)
	Quotation in reply from a local council official.
5	A final witty comment.

Bill Bryson

1 **a)** What exactly is junk food? Talk in a group about the kind of junk food that you eat (or refuse to eat) and why it is popular.

b) Hold a class debate about junk food. One side argues that it is convenient and fun; the other side that it is bad for you and disgusting to eat.

2 Bill Bryson's account of buying and using up junk food would make a successful episode for a situation comedy. Much of the dialogue is already there.

Draft a television version of the trip to the supermarket. Begin with Bryson's discovery of the junk food section – 'It was heaven', and write a brief description of each shot. You will need to describe both what is happening (*walking down the cereal aisle*) and how it is happening (*grabs, sprints, disapprovingly*). For example, you might start like this:

SHOT 1: BRYSON WALKING DOWN THE CEREAL AISLE. CEREALS HAVE ALL SORTS OF DISGUSTING NAMES (SUCH AS . . .).

SHOT 2: HE GRABS PACKETS OF . . .

SHOT 3: HE SPRINTS WITH HIS CEREALS BACK TO THE TROLLEY. HIS WIFE LOOKS AT THEM.

WIFE (*disapprovingly*): What's that?

BRYSON (*dashing past*): Breakfast for the next six months . . . and don't . . .

Laurie Lee

1　Look back at Laurie Lee's description of his first day at school (from 'This school . . .' to '. . . my potato.'). Find the following words and talk together about the ways in which Lee uses them.

　　adjectives to convey how strange and overpowering everything seemed:
　　wild • outlying • half-hidden • strange • quaint • amazed • tall • huge • hideous.
　　verbs to convey how rough and violent the new experience seemed:
　　swept　　　down • confronted • surrounded • thrust • picked up • roared • burned • skating and skidding • closed　　in • encircled • prod • plucked • spun • screwed • stole.

2　**a)**　Find the places where Lee uses direct speech (the characters' own words) and act them out as though they were part of the dialogue in a play. You could begin:
　　　　LAURIE (*looking at the potato*): What's this?
　　　　SISTER: You're starting school today.
　　　　LAURIE: I ain't. I'm stopping 'ome.

　　b)　Then redraft the direct speech as reported speech ('Laurie looked at the potato and asked what it was').

　　c)　Why do you think Lee chose to give the characters' actual words?

3　Talk in groups about your earliest memories of primary, infants or nursery school. Then, on your own, write an account of your earliest days at school.

Try to use:

- adjectives (to describe the strangeness of it all)
- verbs (to get across the idea of all the activity and bustle)
- direct speech (to let the reader 'hear' exactly what people said).

Emmeline Pankhurst

1 The demonstrations of 1 March had been carefully planned in advance, and the police were taken completely by surprise. To help you understand exactly what was planned and what the order of events was, answer the following questions in pairs:

a) How did the suffragettes disguise the fact that they were planning a demonstration on 1 March?
b) Where did Emmeline Pankhurst go on the Friday afternoon?
c) What did they do at half-past five?
d) What happened to them as a result?
e) What then happened throughout central London?
f) Which streets were affected, for example?
g) How long did the demonstration last?
h) How many suffragettes were arrested over the two days?

2 In note form, write a detailed outline of the 'battle-plan' that Emmeline Pankhurst and her fellow suffragettes might have drawn up in the spring of 1907.
You might begin:

> 1. Let the police know that we are planning a demonstration on 4 March.
> 2. Finalise plans for an unannounced demonstration on 1 March:
>   (i) late afternoon, take taxi to . . .

3 Use an encyclopedia or a history textbook to find out more about the suffragettes. Then discuss as a class whether you think they were justified in breaking the law.

Mary Seacole

Imagine you are one of the nurses or doctors working alongside Mary Seacole at the battle of Tchernaya. Write a letter to a friend at home, describing her work and giving a good idea of the kind of woman she is. Pick out several incidents and comments from the extract to support what you choose to say about her.

You might begin:

> **Mrs Seacole continues to do amazing work here among the wounded and dying soldiers . . .**

You could say something about:

- her presence on the battlefield
- her treatment of enemy Russians as well as British and allied soldiers
- her reaction to the incident involving the soldier with a musket-ball lodged in his mouth
- the soldiers who thanked her
- the Cossack colt.

Comparing the extracts

1 Different autobiographies have different purposes: some are mainly attempting to entertain you; others have a more educational purpose. This can make it difficult to compare one autobiography with another. Complete the grid below, making a note of what you think the *main* purpose of each extract was; you might find two or more main purposes in some of them. For example, one of the main purposes might have been:

- to help the reader picture a scene or event
- to entertain the reader
- to give the reader information
- to describe what happened
- to express an opinion and persuade you to agree with it
- to do something else (if so, what?).

| Extract | Main Purposes | | | | | |
	Picturing scene or event	Entertain-ment	Information	Description of event	Persuasion	Other
Tom Baker						
Gerald Durrell						
Clive James						
Bill Bryson						
Laurie Lee						
Emmeline Pankhurst						
Mary Seacole						

2 You are going to write a short piece from your own autobiography. First of all, decide on what you want to write about. It might be:

- events that you enjoyed at the time (like Tom Baker)
- something that was very dangerous, but is funny to look back on (like Gerald Durrell)
- a humorous situation (like Clive James)
- something amusing about your lifestyle (like Bill Bryson)
- impressions from your earliest days at school (like Laurie Lee)
- an exciting and action-packed moment (like Emmeline Pankhurst)
- vivid impressions of an event you took part in (like Mary Seacole)

Then, think carefully about the main purpose of your writing (to entertain the reader, to provide information, or . . . ?)

Section 3
DIARIES

Have you ever kept a diary? If you have, you probably
didn't want other people to read it. Many people,
though, keep diaries as records of the times they are
living through. They try to make them as detailed and
exciting as possible, in the hope that one day other
people will read them and will once again become
involved in the powerful stories they tell. Sometimes
diaries record dramatic, life-and-death adventures,
such as Captain Scott's journal of his ill-fated trek to the
South Pole. At other times, they deal with nothing more
life-threatening than the sea of mud at a Glastonbury
rock festival.

Jim Parton

Jim Parton wasn't a great fan of rock or pop until he was asked to write a book about Robbie Williams. But, although he ended up a fan, following the singer round the country for a year wasn't all fun. In this extract from his diary of the tour, the bus carrying Robbie Williams's team arrives for a performance at the Glastonbury festival – only to find that the whole site is covered in deep, thick mud. Williams' last appearance at Glastonbury had not been a happy one (he had appeared unexpectedly with Oasis on stage, having been drinking in their tent beforehand).

Saturday morning; arriving at Glastonbury it's rain, rain, rain. Andy Franks [Williams' tour manager], logistical genius that he is, has managed to get the bus to pull up outside a fishing tackle shop, where the entire crew have been equipped with waders and wellies.

Inside the bus there is a strict no-shoes rule to try to keep it civilised. The occupants of some of the tents on the surrounding hillside have attempted to impose similar discipline. Every occupied tent has a pair of muddy legs sticking out of the front door (can't be bothered to take the boots off), with people trying to keep the inside clean. It's a hopeless battle.

There is still some sign that the tents were originally pitched in grassy meadows. But with each footstep new mud is released, and around the sound stages there is enough of it to shame the

Somme: First World War battlefield, notorious for its mud

battlefields of the **Somme**. It flows down the hill in rivulets, and unless you have a very good groundsheet it must be impossible to stay clean or dry. If you're lucky enough to own wellingtons it is risky to leave them outside your tent.

A minority have come equipped with wellingtons. The rest either accept that they're going to have wet feet, or try to hop from dry patch to dry patch, before giving up and accepting their fate. A lot of people have Sainsbury's bags tied round their ankles. Good try, but hopeless.

The weather is strange. Torrential downpour followed by shafts of brilliant sunlight, cutting through mountainous white clouds tinged with angry grey, reflecting off the gleaming tents and the mud. The scene acquires an unexpected beauty.

When the sun comes out there's a crowd of nutters rolling in the mud. I suppose it's a case of 'if you can't beat it, roll in it.'

Back in the bus, Chris Shorrock [Williams's drummer]'s ten-year-old son is sprawling on the floor. He's bored, there's nothing to do. Normally he would be out playing football with other kids, or with the band, which has quite a keen five-a-side team.

Robbie arrives from London in the middle of the afternoon with Nicky [his fiancée] and Jan [his mother]. His Range Rover is perfect for the conditions, although it doesn't normally get much of a chance to get muddy. In fact it still looks like a new car, apart from a muddy hand print on the blackened window, put there by a fan who wanted to stare in.

Nicky describes how her mother took her to a muddy rock festival back in Canada. She's quite funny talking about it, and you get the impression she'd have liked to have been out there sliding around in the mud, if the price of fame hadn't forced her to stay in the nice warm bus.

Then, almost imperceptibly the relaxed atmosphere inside the bus begins to change. There's less chat, less banter. Robbie doesn't look nervous, but there's something different about him, so he must be nervous. Terrified is more like it. This is the biggest gig of his life. The crowd isn't coming to see five members of a boy band. They're coming to see just him, and he's got to entertain them.

Vocal warm-ups for the band start in the back of the bus, led by Guy [Guy Chambers: musical director, co-writer and keyboard player], arpeggios up and down in different keys. The same exercises as opera singers; you could forget this was a rock band. By this time Robbie has changed into his stage clothes. There's a quarter of an hour to go, and he has a few interviews to do. He's on duty. He does a television interview; before he answers each question a friend talks into his ear. Robbie comes out with robotic answers, pretending to be a dumb rock star checking with his management what he's allowed to say. It's completely improvised and very funny.

'Stop now, stop now,' he goes, 'Leave me alone, I must go,' and puts a hand up in front of the cameras, before climbing into the Range Rover for the 100-yard drive to the stage. Before you ask, no, he couldn't possibly walk. He'd get his clothes dirty.

Looking down from the stage, a sea of faces stretches into the distance, but the field is not as full as it could be. You can't blame them, it's miserable out there, and it's still a pretty impressive turn out. In the distance people are making their way along a path of World War I duck boards, as if passing from one line of trenches to another, but they're not stopping to see who is about to appear on the main stage.

Then the Star Wars music rings out, and the stage fills with smoke. Almost at that moment a shaft of bright yellow light shines through the clouds, illuminating the whole crowd. The band arrive as 'Let Me Entertain You' starts. The crowd shrieks, then subsides as they realise Robbie hasn't arrived yet. When he does, they all start jumping up and down, and don't stop until the set ends an hour later.

As the set progresses, people passing on the distant duck boards realise something is going on, and begin to turn towards the stage. Robbie shouts to all those still in their tents to come on down. The field begins to fill up.

Just to the side of the stage the 'two proud dads' [Tim Clarke and

David Enthoven: Williams' management team] look happy and, well, proud. They don't watch Robbie performing – they do that all the time anyway. They look at a crowd having the time of its life. Near the front, a couple of girls have gone topless, and are swaying on their boyfriends' shoulders.

There is a ten yard gap between stage and crowd, just enough room to allow the St John's ambulance staff to work. Every so often a collapsed body gets passed across people's heads and handed to the resuscitation crew. You worry that if someone fainted and fell to the ground they would be as likely to drown in the mud as be trampled.

Then quite a nasty fight breaks out, and a boxing ring-size gap opens up in the crowd. Robbie keeps going; maybe he's not seen it, but maybe he's so

professional he can play through it. After a while the **miscreants** melt into the crowd, and a very limp-looking, mud-splattered body is passed to the front. There was nothing in the papers the next day, so he must have been OK.

99.99% of the swelling crowd has missed this excitement and continues to be royally entertained. At one point Robbie gets them singing a chorus of 'Hey Jude'.

At another it's 'Are we going to win on Tuesday?' A huge 'Yes' goes up. (England has a World Cup match.) He starts an unaccompanied chorus of 'Three Lions', then it's back to his own music. The 'two proud dads' are positively beaming now, like you've never seen men beam. Robbie's got this crowd eating out of his hand.

The set ends with 'Angels'. It's an emotional moment; the band stops,

miscreants: wrongdoers

and the crowd carries on with the chorus. They all know it now, it's entered the public consciousness. Then the band rejoins the song, and Robbie gives it a final go.

Back in the bus he sits quietly with his mother and Nicky. He looks drained, not euphoric, almost in state of shock – and perhaps he is – as if he didn't believe he could do it. Glastonbury was where his troubles had started, now he's conquered it, and with it many of the demons that have haunted him over the last few years.

There will be other demons of course; it's the way this insecure man is driven, but it's also the reason he can be an entertainer who appeals across the generations.

In five years' time he could have been thinking over a cigarette, 'I was famous once. What happened?'

Not much chance of that happening now.

Robert Falcon Scott

In 1910, Robert Falcon Scott and a team of Antarctic explorers set out on a historic expedition – hoping to be the first people to set foot at the South Pole. On 18 January 1912, Scott and four companions at last reached their destination, only to be devastated by the discovery that a Norwegian expedition, led by Roald Amundsen, had beaten them to it. Dispirited, they set off for base camp. But, in the punishing conditions, not one was to survive.

Wednesday, January 17. – Camp 69. –22° at start. Night –21°. The Pole. Yes, but under very different circumstances from those expected. We have had a horrible day – add to our disappointment a head wind 4 to 5, with a temperature of –22°, and companions labouring on with cold feet and hands.

We started at 7.30, none of us having slept much after the shock of our discovery. We followed the Norwegian sledge tracks for some way; as far as we make out there are only two men. Then the weather overcast, and the tracks being increasingly drifted up and obviously going too far to the west, we decided to make straight for the Pole according to our calculations. At 12.30 Evans had such cold hands we camped for lunch – an excellent 'week-end one'. We had marched 7.4 miles. Lat. sight gave 89° 53' 37". We started out and did 6½ miles due south. To-night little Bowers is laying himself out to get sights in terrible difficult circumstances; the wind is blowing hard, T. –21°, and there is that curious damp, cold feeling in the air which chills one to the bone in no time. We have been descending again, I think, but there looks to be a rise ahead; otherwise there is very little that is different from the awful monotony of past days. Great God! this is an awful place and terrible enough for us to have laboured to it without the reward of **priority**. Well, it is something to have got here, and the wind may be our friend to-morrow. We have had a fat Polar hoosh in spite of our **chagrin**, and feel comfortable inside – added a small stick of chocolate and the queer taste of a cigarette brought by Wilson. Now for the run home and a desperate struggle. I wonder if we can do it.

Thursday morning, January 18. – Decided after summing up all observations that we were 3.5 miles away from the Pole – one mile beyond it and 3 to the right. More or less in this direction Bowers saw a cairn or tent.

We have just arrived at this tent, 2 miles from our camp, therefore about 1½ miles from the Pole. In the tent we find a record of five Norwegians having been here, as follows:

> Roald Amundsen
> Olav Olavson Bjaaland
> Hilmer Hanssen
> Sverre H. Hassel
> Oscar Wisting.

16 Dec. 1911.

The tent is fine – a small compact affair supported by a single bamboo. A note from Amundsen, which I keep, asks me to forward a letter to King Haakon!

The following articles have been left in the tent: 3 half bags of reindeer containing a miscellaneous assortment of mits and sleeping-socks, very various in description, a **sextant**, a Norwegian artificial horizon

---

priority: being first (to get to the Pole)
chagrin: feeling of great disappointment
sextant: measuring instrument in navigation

and a **hypsometer** without boiling-point thermometers, a sextant and hypsometer of English make.

Left a note to say I had visited the tent with companions. Bowers photographing and Wilson sketching. Since lunch we have marched 6.2 miles S.S.E. by compass (i.e. northwards). We built a cairn, put up our poor slighted Union Jack, and photographed ourselves – mighty cold work all of it – less than ½ mile south we saw stuck up an old underrunner of a sledge. This we commandeered as a yard for a floorcloth sail. I imagine it was intended to mark the exact spot of the Pole as near as the Norwegians could fix it. (Height 9500). A note attached talked of the tent as being 2 miles from the Pole. Wilson keeps the note. There is no doubt that our predecessors have made thoroughly sure of their mark and fully carried out their

hypsometer: instrument for measuring height above sea level

programme. I think the Pole is about 9500 feet in height; this is remarkable, considering that in Lat. 88° we were about 10,500.

We carried the Union Jack about ¾ of a mile north with us and left it on a piece of stick as near as we could fix it. I fancy the Norwegians arrived at the Pole on the 15th Dec. and left on the 17th, ahead of a date quoted by me in London as ideal, viz. Dec. 22. It looks as though the Norwegian party expected colder weather on the summit than they got. Well, we have turned our back now on the goal of our ambition and must face our 800 miles of solid dragging – and goodbye to most of the day-dreams!

Wednesday, March 14. – No doubt about the going downhill, but everything going wrong for us. Yesterday we woke to a strong northerly wind with temp. –37°. Couldn't face it, so remained in camp till 2, then did 5¼ miles. Wanted to march later, but party feeling the cold badly as the breeze (N.) never took off entirely, and as the sun sank the temp. fell. Long time getting supper in dark.

This morning started with southerly breeze, set sail and passed another cairn at good speed; half-way, however, the wind shifted to W. by S. or W.S.W., blew through our wind clothes and into our mits. Poor Wilson horribly cold, could [not] get off ski for some time. Bowers and I practically made camp, and when we got into the tent at last we were all deadly cold. Then temp. now midday down –43° and the wind strong. We *must* go on, but now the making of every camp must be more difficult and dangerous. It must be near the end, but a pretty merciful end. Poor Oates got it again in the foot. I shudder to think what it will be like to-morrow. It is only with greatest pains rest of us keep off frostbite. No idea there would be temperatures like this at this time of year with such winds. Truly awful outside the tent. Must fight it out to the last biscuit, but can't reduce rations.

Friday, March 16 or Saturday 17. – Lost track of dates, but think the last correct. Tragedy all along the line. At lunch, the day before yesterday, poor Titus Oates said he couldn't go on; he proposed we should leave him in his sleeping-bag. That we could not do, and we induced him to come on, on the afternoon march. In spite of its awful nature for him he struggled on and we made a few miles. At night he was worse and we knew the end had come.

Should this be found I want these facts recorded. Oates' last thoughts were of his Mother, but immediately before he took pride in thinking that his regiment would be pleased with the bold way in which he met his death. We can testify to his bravery. He has borne intense suffering for weeks without complaint, and to the very last was able and willing to discuss outside subjects. He did not – would not – give up hope till the very end. He was a brave soul. This was the end. He slept through the night before last, hoping not to wake; but he woke in the morning – yesterday. It was blowing a blizzard. He said, 'I am just going outside and may be some time.' He went out into the blizzard and we have not seen him since.

I take this opportunity of saying that we have stuck to our sick companions to the last. In case of Edgar Evans, when absolutely out of food and he lay insensible, the safety of the remainder seemed to demand his abandonment, but Providence mercifully removed him at this critical moment. He died a natural death, and we did not leave him till two hours after his death. We knew that poor Oates was walking to his death, but though we tried to dissuade him, we knew it was the act of a brave man and an English gentleman. We all hope to meet the end with a similar spirit, and assuredly the end is not far.

I can only write at lunch and then only occasionally. The cold is intense, –40° at midday. My companions are unendingly cheerful, but we are all on the verge of serious

frostbites, and though we constantly talk of fetching through I don't think any one of us believes it in his heart.
Sunday, March 18. – To-day, lunch, we are 21 miles from the depôt. Ill fortune presses, but better may come. We have had more wind and drift from ahead yesterday; had to stop marching; wind N.W., force 4, temp. −35°. No human being could face it, and we are worn out *nearly*.

My right foot has gone, nearly all the toes – two days ago I was proud possessor of best feet. These are the steps of my downfall. Like an ass I mixed a small spoonful of curry powder with my melted **pemmican** – it gave me violent indigestion. I lay awake and in pain all night; woke and felt done on the march; foot went and I didn't know it. A very small measure of neglect and have a foot which is not pleasant to contemplate. Bowers takes first place in condition, but there is not much to choose after all. The others are still confident of getting through – or pretend to be – I don't know! We have the last *half* fill of oil in our **primus** and a very small quantity of spirit – this alone between us and thirst. The wind is fair for the moment, and that is perhaps a fact to help. The mileage would have seemed ridiculously small on our outward journey.
Monday, March 19. – Lunch. We camped with difficulty last night, and were dreadfully cold till after our supper of cold pemmican and biscuit and half a pannikin of cocoa cooked over the spirit. Then, contrary to expectation, we got warm and all slept well. To-day we started in the usual dragging manner. Sledge dreadfully heavy. We are 15½ miles from the depôt and ought to get there in three days. What progress! We have two days' food but barely a day's fuel. All our feet are getting bad – Wilson's best, my right foot worst, left all right.

pemmican: dried food, containing meat
primus: small oil-burning stove

There is no chance to nurse one's feet till we can get hot food into us. Amputation is the least I can hope for now, but will the trouble spread? That is the serious question. The weather doesn't give us a chance – the wind from N. to N.W. and –40° temp. to-day.

Wednesday, March 21. – Got within 11 miles of depôt Monday night; had to lay up all yesterday in severe blizzard. To-day forlorn hope, Wilson and Bowers going to depôt for fuel.

Thursday, March 22 and 23. – Blizzard bad as ever – Wilson and Bowers unable to start – to-morrow last chance – no fuel and only one or two of food left – must be near the end. Have decided it shall be natural – we shall march for the depôt with or without our effects and die in our tracks.

Thursday, March 29. – Since the 21st we have had a continuous gale from W.S.W. and S.W. We had fuel to make two cups of tea apiece and bare food for two days on the 20th. Every day we have been ready to start for our depôt 11 *miles* away, but outside the door of the tent it remains a scene of whirling drift. We shall stick it out to the end, but we are getting weaker, of course, and the end cannot be far.

It seems a pity, but I do not think I can write more.

R. Scott.

Last entry.

For God's sake look after our people.

This diary was found eight months later by a search party, along with the bodies of Scott and his companions.

John Evelyn

John Evelyn was a great traveller and a friend of the more famous diarist, Samuel Pepys. In this entry, for 11 June 1664, he describes one of the major hazards of seventeenth-century travel: highway robbery!

The weather being hot, and having sent my man on before, I rode **negligently** under favour of the shade, till within three miles of Bromley, at a place called the Procession Oak, two cut-throats started out, and striking with long staves at the horse and taking hold of the reins threw me down, took my sword, and **haled** me into a deep thicket some quarter of a mile from the highway, where they might securely rob me, as they soon did. What they got of money was not considerable, but they took two rings, the one an emerald with diamonds, the other an onyx, and a pair of buckles set with rubies and diamonds, which were of value, and after all bound my hands behind me, and my feet, having before pulled off my boots; they then set me up against an oak, with most bloody threats to cut my throat if I **offered** to cry out or make any noise, for they should be within hearing, I not being the person they looked for. I told them if they had not **basely** surprised me they should not have had so easy a prize, and that it would teach me never to ride near a hedge, since had I been in the mid-way they **durst** not have adventured on me; at which they cocked their pistols, and told me they had long guns too, and were 14 companions. My horse's bridle they slipt, and searched the saddle, which they pulled off, but let the horse graze, and then turning again bridled him and

negligently: carelessly   **haled**: dragged   **offered**: attempted
basely: dishonourably   **durst**: dared

tied him to a tree, yet so as he might graze, and thus left me bound. Left in this manner grievously was I tormented with flies, ants, and the sun, nor was my anxiety little how I should get loose in that solitary place, where I could neither hear or see any creature but my poor horse and a few sheep straggling in the copse. After near 2 hours attempting I got my hands to turn palm to palm, having been tied back to back, and then it was long before I could slip the cord over my wrists to my thumb, which at last I did, and then soon unbound my feet, and saddling my horse and roaming awhile about I at last perceived dust to rise, and soon after heard the rattling of a cart, towards which I made, and by the help of two countrymen I got back into the highway. I rode to Col. Blount's, a great justiciary of the times, who sent out hue and cry immediately. The next morning, sore as my wrists and arms were, I went to London and got 500 **tickets** printed and dispersed by an officer of Goldsmiths Hall, and within two days I had tidings of all I had lost except my sword which had a silver hilt and some trifles. The rogues had pawned one of my rings for a trifle to a goldsmith's servant before the tickets had come to the shop, by which means they escaped; the other ring was bought by a **victualler**, who brought it to a goldsmith, but he having seen the ticket seized the man. I afterwards discharged him on his protestation of innocence. Thus did God deliver me from these villains, and not only so, but restored what they took, as twice before he had graciously done, both at sea and land; I mean when I had been robbed by pirates, and was in danger of a considerable loss at Amsterdam; for which, and many, many **signal** preservations, I am extremely obliged to give thanks to God my Saviour.

tickets: handbills
victualler: someone who sells food
signal: notable

Anne Hughes

Some people believe that Anne Hughes's diary is a forgery – a clever fake written in the twentieth century; but many experts are convinced that Anne Hughes was a real farmer's wife who lived in Herefordshire around two centuries ago. This extract, written in Anne's home dialect, is from 23 August 1796.

Aug. ye 23. – Me and Sarah bein bussie with lime washen of the kitchen and house place, John hav to feed the pigges and calfs, which do fuss him much; and the big boar pigg biting him hard on the leg, he cums in most **wrotheful**, and sayes he wil hav us out cum tomorrow. At which I do say how can we when we so bussie? So he off out agen after hitting the cat with my pewter pepper pot.

Then in cums Sarah with her hand all bloddie and she crieing, saying she did do it with the big carver. This I do wash and tye with a peece of old shirt.

John in agen do say whats ado, and me telling him, he mighty cross, saying it be all done apurpus to vex him and not to go out to help him. Indeed he be verrie wrothe.

At this I be so cross I uppes and sayes Sarah be my maid not his, and he to get out of my kitchen till his temper be better. So he out, shutting the door with a grate noise, saying that wimmen was the verrie divvell; at which I so wrothe I did throw a lump of bredd at him, but only hit the shut doore. Then I did pictur to myself Johns face if I had hit him, and fell to laffing so hartilie that the tears

wrotheful: angry

did run adown my cheekes. John do think he be such a grett man, but lord he be just a bigge sillie.

Then me telling Sarah all, she do say: make him a pan cake, and he soone better. So she off to bring sum egges warm from the neste, and we set to makeing agen John do cum in. I did also get out a bottle of my fuzzy [furze or gorse] wine, this bein a grate favourit of his.

Now Sarah who be a **sensie** maid do say, here he cums; and do start to say how happie she be to be living with us and what a good master John is, and her plase here so much better and higher up than anie other farmers place anie ware, and he as good looking gentleman as anie here.

I do look at John from my eye corner and sense he lookes verrie pleased, not knowing it be all apurpus. Then he inside to say give him the paile for to fetch in the egges, which Sarah does.

Later we to supper, and John etting his bellie full do say the fuzzy wine be grand, and to give Sarah a **tott**; she being a good wench and respectful to her betters. This I do, and Sarah did thank him verrie prettie, and wishing him good luck did drunke it uppe.

sensie: quick-witted   **tott**: small drink

ACTIVITIES

Jim Parton

Jim Parton writes his account as an outside observer. Robbie Williams would recall the same events slightly differently: for example, only Robbie Williams himself could say exactly how he felt as he climbed on stage to face a Glastonbury audience again.

Write a section of Robbie Williams's own diary for that day. You don't need to use everything that Jim Parton has written about: make a list of the things which you think would have made the biggest impression on the singer, such as:

- life in the tents and around the field
- the weather
- your preparation in the tour bus
- your television interview
- your performance
- the crowd's reactions and behaviour
- how you felt afterwards, back in the bus.

You could start:

> My main impression when I arrived at Glastonbury with Nicky and Mum was of mud everywhere . . .

Or the same entry in note form might look like this:

> Saturday. Arrived at Glastonbury with Nicky and Mum. Mud everywhere . . .

Robert Falcon Scott

1 In his diary Scott manages to be very matter-of-fact about dramatic events – and that it why it is so powerful. To gain a fuller grasp of just how dramatic the expedition's last days were, answer the following questions in pairs:

- What was the first piece of evidence which told Scott and his companions that they were not going to be the first to reach the South Pole?
- What other evidence did they come across that morning?
- What was the nationality of the first men who did reach the Pole?
- How many were in that team, and who was their leader?
- How did Titus Oates meet his death?
- What were the names of the other men travelling with Scott?

2 **a)** How does Scott manage to convey:

- the sense of disappointment at being beaten to the Pole (look at the entry for Wednesday, 17 January)
- the dreadful conditions (17 January; 14 March and 18 March);
- the heroism of Oates and Evans (16 or 17 March)
- the growing realisation that they are not going to survive (16 or 17 March, and the final entries from 19 March onwards)?

   b) Which details from Scott's diary do you find most impressive? Why?

3 Using the information in Scott's diary and your answers to activity 1, write one of the following:

- a newspaper obituary on Titus Oates
- a radio news report on the finding of Scott's diary and the explorers' bodies
- an extract from a school history text book about the last days of Scott's expedition.

John Evelyn

1 Evelyn's account of the robbery and what happened afterwards is full of incident. Make a list of the main events as Evelyn describes them. (The notes will help you with activities 2 and 3.)

2 The description of the attack by highwaymen is extremely vivid. Imagine you are going to make a film of it. Write an artwork brief for five or six frames of a storyboard and give each frame some lines from Evelyn's account to be used as a commentary. If you find it easier, you could sketch the frames and write Evelyn's lines underneath.

For example, one frame might show Evelyn trying to struggle free of the ropes tying his hands. The brief might read:

SHOT: Evelyn, sitting by a tree next to the road; he is struggling with the ropes tying his hands; the sun is beating down and he is sweating.

SOUND EFFECTS: flies and insects buzzing and droning; Evelyn panting as he tries to wrench his hands free.

VOICE OVER: 'Left in this manner grievously was I tormented with flies, ants, and the sun . . .'

3 Write a radio news report of the robbery. You could include quotations from Evelyn himself and also from other people, such as Colonel Blount, who organised the search, or the goldsmith's servant who gave some money for one of the rings (you will have to make up what other people said).

Anne Hughes

1 'Regional dialect' means a variety of the English language which is spoken by a particular group of people in one area or region. Standard English is itself a dialect, but is used throughout Britain as a kind of neutral dialect that everyone understands. (An accent is the name we give to the way we pronounce words.)

Write down some examples of Anne Hughes's dialect and then in another column, give the modern, standard English versions. (Don't include words which are the same as in standard English, except for their spelling – such as 'bein' ' for 'being'. They probably represent Anne Hughes's accent.) Here is an example to start you off.

1790s Herefordshire dialect	modern equivalent
John hav to	*John has to*

2 It is easy to imagine the scenes in Anne Hughes's farmhouse as a kind of eighteenth-century 'soap'. In groups of four, redraft the scenes she describes as a radio or television playscript, with parts for Anne, John and Sarah. (If it's radio, you could include Anne's voice as a narrator.)

Try to use as much of Anne's lively language as you can and, when you have completed your script, act it out. Anne's diary was written in Herefordshire dialect, but use whichever dialect and accent you find easiest. You could begin something like this:

SCENE 1: *The farmhouse. Anne and Sarah are washing the walls with lime. Suddenly John rushes in, his leg covered in blood.*

JOHN I'll kill that boar! He's bitten me – look! (*Before they can respond:*) I'm not doing that job again – you two can do it yourselves tomorrow.

ANNE: How can we, when we're so busy?

John doesn't answer, but snatches up a pewter pepper pot and hurls it at the cat (who miaows sadly) before storming out.

Comparing the extracts

1 People keep diaries for all sorts of reasons. For example, they might keep a diary:

- in which they secretly write down their private thoughts and feelings
- to record the interesting or difficult times they are living through
- because it will be important for later generations to know exactly what happened
- which they intend to publish as a book for everyone to read.

In groups, discuss what reasons the four diary writers here – Jim Parton, Robert Scott, John Evelyn and Anne Hughes – might have had for keeping their diary. Which parts of each extract do you think the writer might be particularly pleased to know are being read today?

2 Write an extract from the diary of someone you know well (such as a relative or a close friend), or a celebrity like Robbie Williams, or someone from history, such as Scott. Before you begin writing:

- Look at question 1 again, and decide what reason your person might have for keeping their diary
- then make notes on an exciting or amusing episode from the person's life. (You might choose an important few days in a sportsperson's career, for example, or a decisive period for a famous leader in history.)

Section 4
LETTERS

We all enjoy receiving letters, but what makes people write them? In this section you can read a selection of letters by a variety of different people, and from different moments in history. Not all of them are as dramatic as Anne Boleyn's to her husband Henry VIII just a short while before she was beheaded, or Nelson's on the eve of the fateful Battle of Trafalgar. But they all have one thing in common – in times of excitement, anguish or simple irritation, the writer felt the need to write to someone else.

Strong words

Have you ever felt that you wanted to send a letter to someone telling them exactly what you felt? These four letters do just that.

Sir Philip Sidney

In this first letter (written in 1578), Sir Philip Sidney tells his father's secretary, Edmund Molyneux, just what he will do if he catches him opening his letters again. (Poor old Molyneux turned out to be innocent of the charge!)

Mr Molyneux,

Few words are best. My letters to my father have come to the eyes of some: neither can I condemn any but you for it. If it be so, you have played the very **knave** with me: and so I will make you know if I have good proof of it. But that for so much as is past. For that is to come, I assure you before God, that if ever I know you do so much as read any letter I write to my father, without his commandment or my consent, I will thrust my dagger into you. And trust to it, for I speak it in earnest. In the mean time, farewell. From Court, this last of May 1578.

By me
Philip Sidney

knave: a dishonest man

Elizabeth, Queen of Bohemia

Elizabeth of Bohemia (in the modern-day Czech Republic) was the sister of the English King Charles I. In this letter written in 1630, she sends a gentle reminder to the Earl of Carlisle, who seems to have forgotten to write to her.

Thou ugly, filthy, camel's face, You **chid** me once for not writing to you; now I have my revenge, and more justly chide you, for not having heard from you so long as I fear you have forgot to write. I have **charged** this fat fellow to tell you all this, and that I cannot forget your villany. He can inform [you] how all things are here, and what they say to the peace with Spain; and though I confess I am not much rejoiced at it, yet I am so confident of my dear brother's love, and the promise he hath made me, not to **forsake** our cause, that it troubles me the less. I must desire your sweet face to continue your help to us, in this business which concerns me so near; and in spite of you, I am ever constantly

Your most affectionat frend
Elizabeth

chid: chided me, told me off, complained at me
charged: ordered
forsake: desert

James Stanley, Earl of Derby

In the English Civil War the Royalists supported the king; the Roundheads (so called because of their short hair) supported Parliament. This is how the Royalist Earl of Derby reacted in 1649, when Henry Ireton tried to persuade him to join the Roundhead cause.

Sir,

I have received your letter with indignation, and with scorn return you this answer, that I cannot but wonder whence you should gather any hopes that I should prove like you, treacherous to my sovereign; since you cannot be ignorant of the **manifest candour** of my former actings in **his late Majesty's** service, from which principles of loyalty I am **not a whit** departed. I scorn your **proffer**; I disdain your favour; I abhor your treason; and am so far from delivering up this island to your advantage, that I shall keep it to the utmost of my power, and, I hope, to your destruction. Take this for your final answer, and **forbear any further solicitations**; for if you trouble me with any more messages of this nature, I will burn your paper, and hang up your messenger. This is the **immutable** resolution, and shall be the undoubted practice, of him who accounts it his chiefest glory to be his Majesty's most loyal and obedient subject,

Derby

manifest candour: obvious frankness and honesty
his late Majesty: the king who had recently died (Charles I had been executed earlier that same year)
not a whit: not in the slightest bit
proffer: offer
forbear any further solicitations: don't try to talk me round any more
immutable: unchangeable

George Bernard Shaw

This letter was written by the playwright George Bernard Shaw to his friend Stella Campbell in 1918. Shaw felt that the Great War, or First World War, was a terrible waste of life and reacted angrily when Stella Campbell wrote to tell him that her son had been killed in action. Shaw felt particularly bitter that she had described the letter from her son's army chaplain as being 'full of tragic gentleness'.

Never saw it or heard about it until your letter came. It is no use: I **cant** be sympathetic: these things simply make me furious. I want to swear. I *do* swear. Killed just because people are blasted fools. A chaplain, too, to say nice things about it. It is not his business to say nice things about it, but to shout that 'the voice of thy son's blood crieth unto God from the ground.'

To hell with your chaplain and his tragic gentleness! The next shell will perhaps blow *him* to bits; and some other chaplain will write such a nice letter to *his* mother. Such nice letters! Such nice little notices in papers!

Gratifying, isnt it. Consoling. It only needs a letter from the king to make me feel that the shell was a blessing in disguise.

No: dont show me the letter. But I should very much like to have a nice talk with that dear chaplain, that sweet sky pilot, that – No use going on like this,

cant: can't (Shaw was against using apostrophes)

Stella. Wait for a week; and then I shall be very clever and broadminded again, and have forgotten all about him. I shall be quite as nice as the chaplain.

Oh damn, damn, damn, damn, damn, damn, damn, damn, DAMN

DAMN!

And oh, dear, dear, dear, dear, dear, dearest!
G.B.S.

Life and death

Letters can be literally matters of life and death. When Anne Boleyn wrote the letter below, she was about to be executed; Nelson's was written the day before his death in battle; and Einstein had become aware of the awesome destructive power of nuclear weapons.

Anne Boleyn

Anne Boleyn was Henry VIII's second wife. When he needed an excuse to get rid of her, he accused her of adultery (sexual intercourse with another man) and she was found guilty of high treason, the worst kind of disloyalty to the Crown. This letter was written by Anne to Henry in 1536, shortly before she was beheaded.

Sir, – Your Grace's displeasure, and my imprisonment, are things so strange unto me, as what to write, or what to excuse, I am altogether ignorant. Whereas you send unto me (willing me to
5 confess a truth, and so obtain your favour) by such a one, whom you know to be mine ancient **professed** enemy, I no sooner received this message by him, that I rightly conceived your meaning; and if, as you say, confessing a truth
10 indeed may procure my safety, I shall with all willingness and duty perform your command.

professed: openly declared

But let not your Grace ever imagine that your poor wife will ever be brought to acknowledge a fault, where not so much as a thought thereof preceded. And to speak a truth, never Prince had wife more loyal in all duty, and in all true affection, than you have ever found in Anne Boleyn; with which name and place I could willingly have contented myself, if God and your Grace's pleasure had been so pleased. Neither did I at any time so far forget myself in my **exaltation** or received Queenship, but that I always looked for such an alteration as I now find; for the ground of my **preferment** being on no surer foundation than your Grace's fancy, the least alteration, I knew, was fit and sufficient to draw that fancy to some other object. You have chosen me, from a **low estate**, to be your queen and companion, far beyond my desert or desire. If then, you find me worthy of such honour, good your Grace, let not any light fancy, or bad counsel of mine enemies, withdraw your princely favour from me; neither let that stain, that unworthy stain, of a disloyal heart towards your good Grace, ever cast so foul a blot on your most dutiful wife, and the Infant-Princess your daughter. Try me, good King, but let me have a lawful trial, and let not my sworn enemies sit as my accusers and judges; yea, let me receive an open trial, for my truth shall fear no open shame. Then shall you see either mine innocence cleared, your suspicion and conscience satisfied, the **ignominy** and slander of the world stopped, or my guilt openly declared.

exaltation: high position (as Queen)
low estate: low position socially
preferment: promotion
ignominy: dishonour

But if you have already determined of me, and that
not only my death, but an infamous slander must
bring you the enjoying of your desired happiness;
then I desire of God, that He will pardon your great
sin therein, and likewise mine enemies, the
instruments thereof, and that He will not call you to
a strict account for your unprincely and cruel usage
of me, at his general judgment-seat, where both you
and myself must shortly appear, and in whose
judgment I doubt not (whatsoever the world may
think of me) mine innocence shall be openly and
sufficiently cleared.

My last and only request shall be that myself may
only bear the burden of your Grace's displeasure,
and that it may not touch the innocent souls of those
poor gentlemen who (as I understand) are likewise
in **strait** imprisonment for my sake. If ever I have
found favour in your sight, if ever the name of Anne
Boleyn hath been pleasing in your ears, then let me
obtain this request, and I will so leave to trouble your
Grace any further, with mine earnest prayers to the
Trinity to have your Grace in His good keeping, and
to direct you in all your actions. From my **doleful**
prison in the Tower, this sixth of May.

Your most loyal and ever faithful wife,
Anne Boleyn

strait: strict and severe   **doleful**: unhappy

Horatio Nelson

This letter was the last ever written by Admiral Nelson. He began it two days before the Battle of Trafalgar (fought on 21 October 1805), but did not live to complete it. After his death in battle, the letter was found open on the desk in his cabin and was later delivered by Captain Hardy to Emma, Lady Hamilton, Nelson's mistress.

> Victory Octr. 19th: 1805 Noon Cadiz ESE 16 Leagues
>
> My Dearest beloved Emma the dear friend of my bosom the Signal has been made that the Enemys Combined fleet are coming out of Port. We have very little Wind so that I have no hopes of seeing them before tomorrow May the God of Battles crown my endeavours with success at all events I will take care that my name shall ever be most dear to you and Horatia [their daughter] both of whom I love as much as my own life. and as my last writing before the battle will be to you so I hope in God that I shall live to finish my letter after the Battle. May Heaven bless you prays your **Nelson & Bronte**. Octr. 20th, in the morning we were close to the mouth of the Streights but the Wind had not come far enough to the Westward to allow the **Combined Fleets** to Weather the shoals off Trafalgar but they were

Nelson & Bronte: Nelson's titles were Baron Nelson of the Nile and Duke of Bronte (in Sicily)
Combined Fleets: the French and Spanish navies

counted as far as forty Sail of Ships of War which I suppose to be 34 of the Line and six frigates, a Group of them was seen off the Lighthouse of Cadiz this Morng but it blows so very fresh & thick weather that I rather believe they will go into the Harbour before night. May God Almighty give us success over these fellows and enable us to get a Peace.

Sam

We do not know the surname of the sailor who wrote this letter to his father, but his first name was Sam. He served on board the *Royal Sovereign*, the flagship of Admiral Collingwood, Nelson's second-in-command at Trafalgar.

Honoured Fathre,
This comes to tell you that I am alive and hearty except three fingers; but that's not much, it might have been my head. I told brother Tom I should like to see a **greadly** battle, and I have seen one, and we have peppered the Combined rarely (off Trafalgar); and for the matter of that, they fought us pretty tightish for French and Spanish. Three of our mess are killed, and four more of us winged. But to tell you the truth of it, when the game began, I wished myself at Warnborough with my plough again; but when they had given us one

greadly: great

duster, I found myself snug and tight, I set to in good earnest, and thought no more about being killed than if I were at Murrell Green Fair, and I was presently as busy and as black as a **collier**. How my fingers got knocked overboard I don't know, but off they are, and I never missed them till I wanted them. You see, by my writing, it was my left hand, so I can write to you and fight for my King yet. We have taken a rare parcel of ships, but the wind is so rough we cannot bring them home, else I should roll in money, so we are busy smashin 'em, and blowing 'em up wholesale.

Our dear Admiral Nelson is killed! so we have paid pretty sharply for licking 'em. I never set eyes on him, for which I am both sorry and glad; for to be sure, I should like to have seen him – but then, all the men in our ship are such soft toads, they have done nothing but blast their eyes, and cry, ever since he was killed. God bless you! chaps that fought like the devil, sit down and cry like a wench. I am still in the *Royal Sovereign*, but the Admiral has left her, for she is like a horse without a bridle, so he is in a frigate that he may be here and there and everywhere, for he's as **cute** as here and there one, and as bold as a lion, for all he can cry! I saw his tears with my own eyes, when the boat hailed and said my Lord was dead. So no more at present from

Your dutiful Son,
Sam

---

duster: attack   **collier**: coal-miner   **cute**: clever

Albert Einstein

Albert Einstein, one of the twentieth century's greatest scientists, sent this letter to the President of the United States, Franklin Delano Roosevelt, in 1939. It led to the construction of the world's first atomic bomb.

Albert Einstein
Old Grove Rd.
Nassau Point
Peconic, Long Island
August 2nd, 1939

F. D. Roosevelt
President of the United States
White House
Washington, D.C.

Sir:

Some recent work by E. Fermi and L. Szilard, which has been communicated to me in manuscript, leads me to expect that the element uranium may be turned into a new and important source of energy in the immediate future. Certain aspects of the situation seem to call for watchfulness and, if necessary, quick action on the part of the **administration**. I believe, therefore, that it is my duty to bring to your attention the following facts and recommendations.

In the course of the last four months it has been made probable – through the work of Joliot in France

---

administration: government

as well as Fermi and Szilard in America – that it may become possible to set up nuclear chain reactions in a large mass of uranium, by which vast amounts of power and large quantities of new radium-like elements would be generated. Now it appears almost certain that this could be achieved in the immediate future.

This new phenomenon would also lead to the construction of bombs, and it is conceivable – though much less certain – that extremely powerful bombs of a new type may thus be constructed. A single bomb of this type, carried by boat or exploded in a port, might very well destroy the whole port together with some of the surrounding territory. However, such bombs might very well prove to be too heavy for transportation by air.

The United States has only very poor **ores** of uranium in moderate quantities. There is some good ore in Canada and **the former Czechoslovakia**, while the most important source of uranium is the Belgian Congo.

I understand that Germany has actually stopped the sale of uranium from the Czechoslovakian mines which she has taken over. That she should have taken such early action might perhaps be understood on the ground that the son of the German Undersecretary of State, von Weizsäcker, is attached to the Kaiser Wilhelm Institute of Berlin, where some of the American work on uranium is now being repeated.

Yours very truly,
A. Einstein

---

ores: minerals from which uranium could be extracted
the former Czechoslovakia: Czechoslovakia lost its independence in March 1939 after the Nazi invasion

Irma Borchard

The document printed on these pages was produced by
the Gestapo in July of 1942 and gives instructions about
the transportation of Jews to the concentration camps in
other parts of Germany and eastern Europe. Following it,
you can read a letter sent from a transit camp by Irma
Borchard to her sister, with an added message by her
mother, Johanna Salomon. Irma was about to have
a baby; neither she nor her mother was heard of again.

Department of Rostock. Schwerin,
6.7.1942

Gestapo Headquarters to the Police
Superintendent of Rostock

re. Evacuation of the Jews to the
East.

From 11.7.1942 Jews of the district
will be evacuated to the East.

This order refers to those Jews who
are listed at the end of this document

It is required that a list of their
properties is to be made out and sent
to me by Thursday, 9.7.42 by special
delivery. The Jews are to be informed
that this list of any property or
moneys owned by them is to be written
with great care. For Minors and wives
the head of the household will be
responsible for the list. This is so

even if the Minor or wife have no property of their own. Any documents referring to the listed property are to be attached.

The Jews are to be told that they must take great care with this declaration. Their attention is to be drawn to the fact that they must expect no **leniency** if they do not make the document sufficiently detailed and accurate, and that they may expect the most **stringent punitive measures** by the police if it is subsequently found that there are errors in the statements.

<u>The Jews may take with them</u> the following per person:

1 Suitcase or Rucksack containing:
1 pair of heavy working boots
2 pairs of socks
2 shirts
2 pairs underpants
1 work suit
2 woollen blankets
2 sets of bedlinen
1 eating bowl
1 mug
1 spoon
1 pullover
Food to last three days
50 marks per person

leniency: soft treatment
stringent punitive measures: harsh punishment

<u>Not allowed are</u>

Savings Books, Investment Documents, Other Documents

Any valuables such as gold, silver, platinum (with the exception of wedding rings)

Pets.

Ration books are to be handed in to the local authorities.

Before leaving their homes the Jews are to be searched for any of the above and for any weapons, explosives and poison.

The police are to seal the homes of the Jews after they have departed and ensure that gas, electricity and water are turned off.

The Jews are to be informed that it is useless to take anything not on the list since these things will be taken away from them at **Ludwigslust**.

The Jews are to pay for their train tickets as far as Ludwigslust.

The local Registration Officer is to put 'unknown' beside names of those Jews who are on the departure list.

The Transport will leave Rostock on Friday, 10.7.1942 at 7.01 o'clock.

Ludwigslust: town in northern Germany between Hamburg and Berlin

The Border Police will get in touch with the Rostock Police re providing personnel.

The leader of the Transport from Rostock to Ludwigshafen will be Criminal Asst. Superintendent Schütt. He will remain in Ludwigshafen until the Transport leaves from there on 11.7.42 at 13.39 o'clock.

Signed: Lange
Kommando of the Schutzpolizei, Rostock Confidential!

* * * * *

To the Leaders of District 1—4 for information and further action:

All Jews listed below shall be taken on foot to the Main Station by Guards on 10.7.42.

To arrive at the Station by 6.45am at the latest.

District Leaders to close and seal the homes, keys to be kept in the District for the time being.

Guards to report to Chief Superintendent Schütt by 6.30am at the station.

Ludwigslust, 11.7.42

Dear Herta

The first dreadful night is behind us. Herr Bernhard will bring you this letter. So, I will tell you briefly. We did not get to bed on the last night, but kept packing. In the morning at 5.30 as Berni came down with our cases, three SS men and a police woman came to search us. Mother and I were searched down to our vests. Our cases were emptied so much that we hardly have any change of clothing left, no sewing kit, no toilet articles, no umbrella, or scissors. The Rucksacks had to be left behind. No soap, brush, slippers, stamps, not a penny in our pockets. No medicine for me and then we were driven to the Station like dogs. At the station the Gestapo were a bit nicer, but our flat was sealed by dreadful men. No cushions for me. Here we lie on hard boards and cement in a big hall. Next week it will be the turn of Uncle Hugo and all the old people. Today we leave at about 1. I travel in the Ambulance compartment. As a special favour I was allowed to have some straw, but no pillow, and I vomited the whole time. Why don't we just make an end of it? Uncle Paul's sister and niece took their life a few days ago. What shall we do when winter comes? All the woollen things have gone. Do you think we have been treated right? Read this letter to everyone and greetings to all our friends, I think this is the last sign of life from us. We have not a penny and no more opportunity. They took my nice **etui** and everything. Write to Uncle Hugo. **Tante** Meta is with us. Uncle Fr. is going with the old people. People from prisons and hospitals are with us. Handbag and toilet things are not on the list. Farewell. I hope your fate is better than ours, but we must not be bitter. Greetings from Irma.

etui: a case to hold small items such as tweezers, needles   **Tante**: Aunt

My dear children, a last farewell,

I hope you had my card. This is what is happening to your mother, who was always so correct and upright. Now everything is gone. Why don't I make an end of it? I had to leave behind everything I loved, even the sweets you gave me, the food for the journey, everything, everything.

Here they are all nice and try to make it easier for us, they share with us. They are not all as badly off as we are. Berni can't get enough to eat. Meta is here, too, I feel sorry for her, she is so unpractical. Please write to Uncle Hugo and Aunt Ella. Who knows how long now, they will all be gone. If you want to write to us, write to the Jewish people in Hamburg. We shall probably go to Warsaw. Now, kisses and greetings to the three of you, greetings to all, especially my darling, will I ever see her again? Be a good child, be a joy to your parents and work hard. Omi loved you so.

Twenty-first-century complaints

These letters were written to newspapers at the beginning of the twenty-first century. All three writers are complaining about a feature of modern life that irritates them.

Out of tune

When I was a teenager in the 1930s we used to sing popular music that had words and tunes, such as 'Red Sails in the Sunset', 'Home on the Range' and 'Singing in the Rain'. In the war, songs with tunes continued ('Wish Me Luck', 'Run, Rabbit, Run', etc). But 50 years ago singers began to have sore throats and words and tunes disappeared. Are we ever to have pleasant tunes back?

Geoffrey Watson
Winchester

from *The Guardian*, 6 January 2000

Mobile madness

Out and about these days, it's impossible to ignore the **plethora** of new mobile phone addicts, enjoying the novelty: 'I'm just eating chicken chow mein down the Chinese'; 'I'm just walking up the steps at the station'; 'I'm just walking down the road to post a letter'.

I watched a young woman sitting in an open-air café waiting for her friend to bring their coffee.

As soon as she was alone, she fumbled in her bag and fetched out her mobile.

She was unable to simply sit and enjoy the atmosphere.

Then I realised: the mobile phone has become the 'cigarette' of the 21st century.

Susan Bennett
London

from *The Mail*, 7 January 2000

Working wear

So women are moaning about having to wear skirts to work and men are moaning about wearing ties, cuffs and collars.

Has anyone spared a thought for all the poor schoolgirls like me who have to wear all of these things?

Nikki Jones
Moreton, Merseyside

from *The Sun*, 2 February 2000

plethora: excess

Two voices

Roald Dahl must be one of the most popular children's writers ever, with books such as *Charlie and the Chocolate Factory* and *Danny, Champion of the World*. Charles Dickens is simply one of the most famous English novelists of all time. But they have more things in common than their success as writers, as these letters show.

Roald Dahl

During the Second World War, Roald Dahl served in North Africa as an RAF pilot, an experience he describes in his book *Going Solo*. In September 1940 he climbed into the cockpit of his Gloster Gladiator and set off to join his squadron. Unfortunately he had been given the wrong directions and, failing to locate the airfield, had to make a forced landing in the desert. As his plane touched the ground, it struck a boulder and Dahl just managed to drag himself away from the wreck before it was consumed by flames. He was quite badly injured and at first feared that he had lost his sight; but, as you can see from the telegram and letters which follow, he was soon able to communicate with his mother in England. In this extract from *Going Solo*, Dahl begins by describing the operation after the crash and then includes some of the letters he sent home to his mother.

I was about to have a major operation performed on my face, and the man who was doing it had been a famous Harley Street plastic surgeon before the war, but now he was a Surgeon-Commander in the navy. One of the nurses had told me about his **Harley Street** days that morning. 'You'll be all right with him,' she had said. 'He's a wonderful worker. And it's all free. A job like you're having would be costing you five hundred guineas in **civvy street**.'

'You mean this is the very first time you've ever used this anaesthetic?' I said to the anaesthetist.

This time he didn't answer me directly. 'You'll love it,' he said. 'You go out like a light. You don't even have any sensation of losing consciousness as you do with the others. So here we go. You'll just feel a little prick on the back of your hand.'

I felt the needle going into a vein on the top of my left hand and I lay there waiting for the moment when I could 'go out like a light'.

I was quite unafraid. I have never been frightened by surgeons or of being given an anaesthetic, and to this day, after some sixteen major operations on numerous parts of my body, I still have complete faith in all, or let me say *nearly* all, those men of medicine.

I lay there waiting and waiting and absolutely nothing happened. My bandages had been taken off for the operation, but my eyes were still permanently closed by the swellings on my face. One doctor had told me it was quite possible that my eyes had not been damaged at all. I doubted

Harley Street: street in London famous for the doctors and surgeons who practise there
in civvy street: in civilian life (i.e. not in the armed forces)

that myself. It seemed to me that I had been permanently blinded, and as I lay there in my quiet black room where all sounds, however tiny, had suddenly become twice as loud, I had plenty of time to think about what total blindness would mean in the future. Curiously enough, it did not frighten me. It did not even depress me. In a world where war was all around me and where I had ridden in dangerous little aeroplanes that roared and zoomed and crashed and caught fire, blindness, not to mention life itself, was no longer important. Survival was not something one struggled for any more. I was already beginning to realise that the only way to conduct oneself in a situation where bombs rained down and bullets whizzed past, was to accept the dangers and all the consequences as calmly as possible. Fretting and sweating about it all was not going to help.

The doctor had tried to comfort me by saying that when you have **contusions** and swellings as massive as mine, you have to wait at least until the swellings go down, and the incrustations of blood around the eyelids have come away.

'Give yourself a chance,' he had said. 'Wait until those eyelids are able to open again.'

Having at this moment no eyelids to open and shut, I hoped the anaesthetist wouldn't start thinking that his famous new wonder anaesthetic had put me to sleep when it hadn't. I didn't want them to start before I was ready. 'I'm still awake,' I said.

'I know you are,' he said.

'What's going on?' I heard another man's voice

contusions: bruises

asking. 'Isn't it working?' This, I knew, was the surgeon, the great man from Harley Street.

'It doesn't seem to be having any effect at all,' the anaesthetist said.

'Give him some more.'

'I have, I have,' the anaesthetist answered, and I thought I detected a slightly ruffled edge to the man's voice.

'London said it was the greatest discovery since chloroform,' the surgeon was saying. 'I saw the report myself. Matthews wrote it. Ten seconds, it said, and the patient's out. Simply tell him to count to ten and he's out before he gets to eight, that's what the report said.'

'This patient could have counted to a hundred,' the anaesthetist was saying.

It occurred to me that they were talking to one another as though I wasn't there. I would have been happier if they had kept quiet.

'Well, we can't wait all day,' the surgeon was saying. It was *his* turn to get irritable now. But I did not want my surgeon to get irritable when he was about to perform a delicate operation on my face. He had come into my room the day before and after examining me carefully, he had said, 'We can't have you going about like that for the rest of your life, can we?'

That worried me. It would have worried anyone. 'Like what?' I asked him.

'I am going to give you a lovely new nose,' he had said, patting me on the shoulder. 'You want to have something nice to look at when you open your eyes again, don't you. Did you ever see **Rudolph Valentino** in the cinema?'

Rudolph Valentino: silent-movie star, famous for his good looks

'Yes,' I said.

'I shall model your nose on his,' the surgeon said. 'What do you think of Rudolph Valentino, Sister?'

'He's smashing,' the Sister said.

And now, in the operating theatre, that same surgeon was saying to the anaesthetist, 'I'd forget that pentathol stuff if I were you. We really can't wait any longer. I've got four more on my list this morning.'

'Right!' snapped the anaesthetist. 'Bring me the nitrous oxide.'

I felt the rubber mask being put over my nose and mouth, and soon the blood-red circles began going round and round faster and faster like a series of gigantic scarlet flywheels and then there was an explosion and I knew nothing more.

When I regained consciousness I was back in my room. I lay there for an uncounted number of weeks.

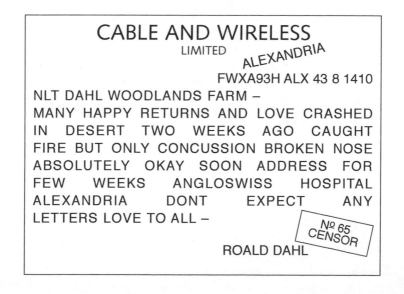

CABLE AND WIRELESS

LIMITED

ALEXANDRIA

FWXA93H ALX 43 8 1410

NLT DAHL WOODLANDS FARM –
MANY HAPPY RETURNS AND LOVE CRASHED IN DESERT TWO WEEKS AGO CAUGHT FIRE BUT ONLY CONCUSSION BROKEN NOSE ABSOLUTELY OKAY SOON ADDRESS FOR FEW WEEKS ANGLOSWISS HOSPITAL ALEXANDRIA DONT EXPECT ANY LETTERS LOVE TO ALL –

No 65 CENSOR

ROALD DAHL

Alexandria
20 November 1940

Dear Mama,

I sent you a telegram yesterday saying that I'd got up for 2 hours & had a bath – so you'll see I'm making good progress. I arrived here about 8½ weeks ago, and was lying on my back for 7 weeks doing nothing, then sat up gradually, and now I am walking about a bit. When I came in I was a bit of a mess. My eyes didn't open (although I was always quite conscious). They thought I had a fractured base (skull), but I think the Xray showed I didn't. My nose was bashed in, but they've got the most marvellous Harley Street specialists out here who've joined up for the war as Majors, and the ear nose & throat man pulled my nose out of the back of my head, and shaped it and now it looks just as before except that it's a little bent about. That was of course under a general anaesthetic.

My eyes still ache if I read or write too much, but they say that they think they'll get back to normal again, and that I'll be fit for flying in about 3 months. In between I still have about 6 or more weeks sick leave here in Alex when I get out, doing nothing in a marvellous sunny climate, just like an English Summer, except that the sun shines every day.

I suppose you want to know how I crashed. Well, I'm not allowed to give you any details of what I was doing or how it happened. But it occurred in the night not very far from the Italian front lines. The plane was on fire and after it hit the ground I was sufficiently conscious to crawl out in time, having undone my straps, and roll on the ground to put out the fire on

Alexandria: city in northern Egypt (often called Alex)

my overalls which were alight. I wasn't burnt much, but was bleeding rather badly from the head. Anyway I lay there and waited for the ammunition which was left in my guns to go off. One after the other, well over 1000 rounds exploded and the bullets whistled about seeming to hit everything but me.

I've never fainted yet, and I think it was this tendency to remain conscious which saved me from being roasted.

Anyway luckily one of our forward patrols saw the blaze, and after some time arrived and picked me up & after much ado I arrived at Mersa Matruh, (you'll see it on the map – on the coast, East of Libya). There I heard a doctor say, 'Oh, he's an Italian is he' (my white flying overalls weren't very recognisable). I told him not to be a **B.F.**, and he gave me some morphia. In about 24 hours time I arrived where I am now, living in great luxury with lots of very nice English nursing sisters to look after me . . .

P.S. The air raids here don't worry us. **The Italians are very bad bombaimers**.

Alexandria
6 December 1940

Dear Mama,

I haven't written to you since my one and only letter some weeks ago, chiefly because the doctors said that it wasn't good for me. As a matter of fact I've been progressing very slowly. As I told you in my telegram I did start getting up, but they soon

---

B.F.: bloody fool
The Italians are very bad bombaimers: the Italian bombing raids were not very accurate

popped me back to bed again because I got such terrific headaches. A week ago I was moved back into this private room, and I have just completed a whole long 7 days lying flat on my back in semi darkness doing absolutely nothing – not even allowed to lift a finger to wash myself. Well, that's over, and I'm sitting up today, (it's 8 o'clock in the evening actually) and writing this and incidentally feeling fine. Tomorrow I think they are going to give me **intravenal saline** injections & make me drink gallons of water – it's another stunt to get rid of the headaches. You needn't be alarmed – there's nothing very wrong with me, I've merely had an extremely serious concussion. They say I certainly won't fly for about 6 months, and last week were going to invalid me home on the next convoy. But somehow I didn't want to – once invalided home, I knew I'd never get on to flying again, and who wants to be invalided home anyway. When I go I want to go normally . . .

Ismailia
12 April 1941

Dear Mama,
A very short note to say that I'm going north across the sea almost at once to join my squadron. I telegraphed this to you today & told you where to send my letters. You may not hear from me for quite a long while so don't worry . . .

intravenal: into the veins   **saline**: salt solution

Alexandria
15 May 1941

Dear Mama,

Well, I don't know what news I can give you. We really had the hell of a time in Greece. It wasn't much fun taking on half the German Airforce with literally a handfull of fighters. My machine was shot up quite a bit but I always managed to get back. The difficulty was choosing a time to land when the German fighters weren't **ground straffing** our aerodrome. Later on we hopped from place to place trying to cover the evacuation – hiding our planes in olive groves and covering them with olive branches in a fairly fruitless endeavour to prevent them being spotted by one or other of the swarms of aircraft overhead. Anyway I don't think anything as bad as that will happen again . . .

Haifa, Palestine
28 June 1941

Dear Mama,

We've been doing some pretty intensive flying just lately – you may have heard about it a little on the wireless. Sometimes I've been doing as much as 7 hours a day, which is a lot in a fighter. Anyway, my head didn't take it any too well, and for the last 3 days I've been off flying. I may have to have another medical board & see if I'm really fit to fly out there. They may even send me to England,

ground straffing: constantly sweeping the ground with gunfire which wouldn't be a bad thing, would it. It's a pity in a way though, because I've just got going. I've got **5 confirmed**, four Germans and one French, and quite a few unconfirmed – and lots on the ground from groundstraffing landing grounds. We've lost 4 pilots killed in the Squadron in the last 2 weeks, shot down by the French. Otherwise this country is great fun and definitely flowing with milk and honey . . .

Charles Dickens

The first of Dickens's letters in this section was written in 1841 to a painter friend, Daniel Maclise. It tells of the death of a pet raven (it had eaten some paint, which in those days contained lead).

12 March 1841

My Dear Maclise,
You will be greatly shocked and grieved to hear that the Raven is no more.

He expired to-day at a few minutes after Twelve o'Clock at noon. He had been ailing (as I told you t'other night) for a few days, but we anticipated no serious result, **conjecturing** that a portion of the white paint he swallowed last summer might be

5 confirmed: the RAF had officially recognised that he had shot down five enemy aircraft
conjecturing: supposing, guessing

lingering about his **vitals** without having any serious effect upon his constitution. Yesterday afternoon he was taken so much worse that I sent an express for the medical gentleman (Mr Herring) who promptly attended, and administered a powerful dose of castor oil. Under the influence of this medicine, he recovered so far as to be able at 8 o'Clock p.m. to bite **Topping**. His night was peaceful. This morning at daybreak he appeared better; received (agreeably to the doctor's directions) another dose of castor oil; and partook plentifully of some warm gruel, the flavour of which he appeared to relish. Towards eleven o'Clock he was so much worse that it was found necessary to **muffle the stable knocker**. At half past, or thereabouts, he was heard talking to himself about the horse and Topping's family, and to add some incoherent expressions which are supposed to have been either a foreboding of his approaching **dissolution**, or some wishes relative to the disposal of his little property – consisting chiefly of halfpence which he had buried in different parts of the garden. On the clock striking twelve he appeared slightly agitated, but he soon recovered, walked twice or thrice along the coach-house, stopped to bark, staggered, exclaimed 'Halloa old girl!' (his favourite expression) and died.

He behaved throughout with a decent fortitude, equanimity, and self-possession, which cannot be too much admired. I deeply regret that being in ignorance of his danger I did not attend to receive

vitals: main organs inside the body
Topping: Dickens's coachman
muffle the stable knocker: muffling doorknockers, to deaden their noise, was a sign that someone in the house was on their deathbed
dissolution: death

his last instructions. Something remarkable about his eyes occasioned Topping to run for the doctor at Twelve. When they returned together our friend was gone. It was the medical gentleman who informed me of his decease. He did it with great caution and delicacy, preparing me by the remark that 'a jolly queer start had taken place', but the shock was very great notwithstanding.

I am not wholly free from suspicions of poison – a malicious butcher has been heard to say that he would 'do' for him – his plea was, that he would not be **molested in taking orders** down the Mews, by any bird that wore a tail – other persons had also been heard to threaten – among others, Charles Knight who has just started a weekly publication, price fourpence; Barnaby being, as you know, Threepence. I have directed a post mortem examination, and the body has been removed to Mr Herring's school of Anatomy for that purpose.

I could wish, if you can take the trouble, that you would inclose this to **Forster** when you have read it. I cannot discharge the painful task of communication more than once. Were they Ravens who took Manna to somebody in the wilderness? At times I hope they were, and at others I fear that they were not, or they would certainly have stolen it by the way.

In profound sorrow, I am ever Your **bereaved** friend.
CD

Kate is as well as can be expected, but terribly low as you may suppose. The children seem rather glad of it. He bit their ancles. But that was play –

molested in taking orders: interfered with when making deliveries
Forster: Dickens' close friend and biographer
bereaved: deprived of someone through their death

The railway accident that Dickens describes in his letter to Thomas Mitton (who had once worked with Dickens as a clerk in a solicitor's office) happened in June 1865. A train from London to Folkestone was derailed and fell into a stream; although Dickens himself was uninjured, ten people died in the crash.

13 June 1865

My dear Mitton

I should have written to you yesterday or the day before, if I had been quite up to writing.

I was in the only carriage that did not go over into the stream. It was caught upon the turn by some of the ruin of the bridge, and hung suspended and balanced in an apparently impossible manner. Two ladies were my fellow-passengers, an old one and a young one. This is exactly what passed. You may judge from it the precise length of the suspense: Suddenly we were off the rail, and beating the ground as the car of a half-emptied balloon might. The old lady cried out, 'My God!' and the young one screamed. I caught hold of them both (the old lady sat opposite and the young one on my left), and said: 'We can't help ourselves, but we can be quiet and composed. Pray don't cry out.' The old lady immediately answered: 'Thank you. Rely upon me. Upon my soul I will be quiet.' We were then all tilted down together in a corner of the carriage, and stopped. I said to them thereupon: 'You may be sure nothing worse can happen. Our danger *must* be over. Will you remain here without stirring, while I get out of the window?' They both answered quite **collectedly**, 'Yes,' and I got out without the least notion what had happened. Fortunately I got out with great caution and stood upon the step. Looking down I saw the bridge had gone, and nothing below me but the line of rail. Some people in the two other compartments were madly trying to plunge out of window, and had no idea that there was an open swampy field fifteen feet down below then, and nothing else! The two guards (one with his face cut) were running up and down on the down side of the bridge (which was not torn up) quite wildly. I called out to them: 'Look at me. Do stop an instant and look at me, and tell me whether you don't know me.' One of them answered: 'We know you very well, Mr Dickens.' 'Then,' I said, 'my good fellow, for God's sake give me your key, and send one of those labourers here, and I'll empty this carriage.' We did it quite safely, by means of a plank or two, and when it was done I saw all the rest of the train, except the two baggage vans, down in the stream. I got into the carriage again for my brandy flask, took off my travelling hat for a basin, climbed down the brickwork, and filled my hat with water.

Suddenly I came upon a staggering man covered with blood (I think he must have been flung clean out of his carriage), with such a frightful cut across the skull that I couldn't bear to look at him. I poured some water over his face and gave him some drink, then gave him some brandy, and laid him down on the grass, and he said, 'I am gone,' and died

collectedly: calmly

afterwards. Then I stumbled over a lady lying on her back against a little pollard-tree, with the blood streaming over her face (which was lead colour) in a number of distinct little streams from the head. I asked her if she could swallow a little brandy and she just nodded, and I gave her some and left her for somebody else. The next time I passed her she was dead. Then a man, examined at the inquest yesterday (who evidently had not the least remembrance of what really passed) came running up to me and implored me to help him find his wife, who afterwards was found dead. No imagination can conceive the ruin of the carriages, or the extraordinary weights under which the people were lying, or the complications into which they were twisted up among iron and wood, and mud and water.

I don't want to be examined at the inquest and I don't want to write about it. I could do no good either way, and I could only seem to speak about myself, which, of course, I would rather not do. I am keeping very quiet here. I have a – I don't know what to call it – **constitutional (I suppose) presence of mind**, and was not in the least fluttered at the time. I instantly remembered that I had the **MS. of a number** with me, and clambered back into the carriage for it. But in writing these scanty words of recollection I feel the shake and am obliged to stop.

                                        Ever faithfully.

---

constitutional...presence of mind: the healthy ability to stay calm in difficult situations
MS. of a number: the manuscript of an issue of *All the Year Round*, which Dickens edited

ACTIVITIES

Strong words

1 The language used by each of the letter-writers is very different. Work on these questions in pairs:

a) Sidney uses simple, mainly monosyllabic words (words of one syllable, such as 'you' and 'know'). His letter contains about 120 words.
- how many are monosyllables?
- what effect does the large number of monosyllabic words have?

b) Elizabeth of Bohemia uses insults in an affectionate letter (look at her changing descriptions of Carlisle's face, for example). Pick out your favourite example and explain to your partner why you like it.

c) Derby uses balanced sentences to express his disgust at Ireton's suggestions. Look at the beginning of the second sentence where he uses three powerful verbs: scorn . . . disdain . . . abhor . . . Use a dictionary to check their meanings. Then write your own balanced sentence opposing another person's point of view, using three equally powerful verbs (for example, hate, reject, despise . . .). Choose a subject you feel strongly about (such as animal rights or capital punishment).

d) Shaw uses informal, colloquial (everyday) language which sounds like spoken English. In pairs, pick out three examples of his colloquial language and redraft it into formal English. Which version do you prefer in each case? Why do you think Shaw chose to use colloquial English?

2 Write your own letter in which you either **a)** threaten what you will do if someone reads your post again, **b)** complain to someone for not having written for a long time, **c)** refuse to do something which someone has been trying to persuade you to do for a long time or **d)** express your feelings about something that makes you angry.

Try to use some of the techniques and language you talked about in activity 1.

Life and Death

Anne Boleyn

1 Imagine that one of Anne Boleyn's ladies-in-waiting is asking her about her imprisonment (obviously she will not have seen the letter that Anne wrote to Henry). Use the points in Anne's letter to answer the following questions in your own words.

a) Who delivered the King's letter to you? What did you feel when you saw who it was? (lines 5–7)

b) Have you been loyal and faithful to the King? (lines 14–17)

c) Did you expect that the King might change in his affections towards you? You are Queen, after all. (lines 18–24)

d) What kind of trial do you expect, and what kind do you hope for? (lines 36–39)

e) Do you hope that the King will be punished by God for mistreating you in this way? (lines 44–52)

f) What do you hope will happen to the men who are accused with you? (lines 50–54)

2 How would you describe the *tone* of Anne's letter? Look back at the following phrases.

- 'Your Grace's displeasure . . . ignorant.' (lines 1-3)
- 'never Prince had wife . . . Anne Boleyn' (lines 14–16)
- 'Try me, good King, but let me have a lawful trial' (lines 32–33)
- 'I desire God that he will pardon your great sin' (lines 41–42)
- 'My last and only . . . displeasure' (lines 56–60).

Is she angry, for example, or bitter, or regretful?

Does she seem to be pleading with Henry and begging for mercy, or merely stating her case?

Nelson and Sam

1 One of these letters was written before the Battle of Trafalgar and one was written after it. Nelson's and Sam's reasons for writing were different too.

a) What do you think their main purpose might have been when they each started to write their letter?

b) Imagine that Nelson and Sam jotted down a few notes before writing their letters. Nelson's might begin:

> Signal received . . . Wind . . . Emma and Horatia . . .

Complete Nelson's notes and draft some notes for Sam's letter. Remember the different audiences and purposes of each letter.

2 **a)** Who would you say was the better letter-writer, Nelson or Sam? Why?

b) Which of the two letters do you find the more interesting? (Think about the particular facts each of the writers has chosen to include, and the details which bring the letters to life.)

c) Who seems to have the better command of English? For example, who is better at:
- spelling and punctuation
- structuring the letter into clear sections, making it easy to read
- choosing vivid words and phrases?

Albert Einstein

When Einstein sent this letter, war between Britain and Germany was already inevitable, though it was not officially declared until a month later – 3 September 1939. Imagine that you are a journalist and have been sent a 'leaked' copy of Einstein's letter only a day or two after it reached the President. Write an article in which you reveal its contents and discuss what might be done. Decide first what kind of newspaper you are writing for – tabloid or broadsheet.

You could include the following facts:
- scientific research is being carried out . . . uranium might soon become a source of energy
- it might be possible to set up nuclear chain reactions . . . this could happen in the immediate future
- this process could lead to the construction of extremely powerful bombs

- the United States does not have much uranium ore, but there is some in Canada . . . Germany has already stopped exporting uranium.

Einstein asks for 'quick action'. You could suggest that a number of steps might be taken, such as:

- arranging an immediate meeting with the scientists
- making a deal with Canada for its uranium ore
- finding out what the German scientists are doing
- keeping all developments from now on totally secret.

Irma Borchard

When we read documents such as the typed Gestapo order and Irma Borchard's letter, it is often the ordinary day-to-day details which are the most moving. What would you have found hardest if you were in Irma's position? Would it be the loss of what you had to leave behind? Parting from friends? The fear of the unknown fate awaiting you? Or other things? Imagine that it is 1942 and that the Gestapo document applies to you.

1 In small groups, talk about:

- some of the practical arrangements you would have to make (to do with travel, packing and money, for example)
- the things it would be painful to leave behind (such as pets, treasured possessions)
- the mixture of feelings you might be experiencing (fear, anger . . .).

2 In the same groups, talk about the differences between the official arrangements outlined in the Gestapo document and what actually happened to Irma Borchard and millions like her. Bring in the facts from Irma's letter (and any knowledge you have from studying the Holocaust at school, or watching films such as *Schindler's List*).

Twenty-first century complaints

1   Choose one of the letters and think about what you would say to the writer if you met them – would you:

- give examples of some of the great songs composed in the last few years
- explain the advantages of mobile phones
- put forward your own views about school uniform?

Now write a letter to them, using this writing frame.

---

your address:

the name and address of the
person you are writing to:

date

Dear Sir/Madam or the person's name

Introductory paragraph
- **I have read your letter about . . .'**
- give a general response to it (agree? disagree?)

Main paragraph
- give two or three reasons in support of your argument

Concluding paragraph
- a final, general point which sums up your argument (you could end with a witty or clever comment, as the writers of the three letters do).

Yours sincerely,/faithfully,

If you begin **Dear Sir** *or* **Dear Madam,** *you end* **Yours faithfully**
If you use their name (**Dear Mrs Smith, Dear Dr Jones,** *etc.*), *you end* **Yours sincerely.**

Sign your name and then print it (or type it) below.

---

2   Think of something which annoys or irritates you, and which might annoy or irritate others too. Then write your own letter to a newspaper about it. Keep it fairly short and to the point – there will be more chance of the newspaper publishing it.

Two voices:
the letters of Dahl and Dickens

Roald Dahl

1 Re-read Dahl's account of his injuries and the operation (pages 117–120), and then compare it with the telegram on page 120 and the letter he sent home on 20 November 1940.

a) Fill in the following grid, which will help you to pick out what information he decides to give his mother in the telegram and first letter, and what he chooses to keep back from her. To help you, the first point has been filled in.

Information given in autobiography	Tick here if he includes it in his telegram and the first letter
The operation was performed by a famous plastic surgeon	✓

b) Look at the points which have not been ticked. Why do you think Dahl chose to leave them out of his telegram? One obvious answer is that there wasn't room; but why choose these points to leave out, rather than others?

2 What tone (or mixture of tones) does Dahl use in his letters? Try to find points at which he is:

- light-hearted
- matter-of-fact
- dramatic
- concerned.

What do the letters reveal about Roald Dahl's personality?

Charles Dickens

1 **a)** Re-read the letters written by Charles Dickens (pages 125–130) and make notes on what he writes about. Use the following headings:

- Dickens's home life and the people in the household
- Dickens's travels and views on people from other countries
- travel and transport
- people's behaviour in extreme situations
- Dickens's family.

b) In pairs, talk together about what you have learned about Charles Dickens and his world.

2 Look carefully at Dickens's letter about the train crash (pages 128–130).

Pick out examples of the following, and then, in pairs, talk about the ways in which each one helps to make the account dramatic:

- dialogue
- vivid details
- description of dramatic moments and incidents
- the expression of Dickens's personal feelings.

Dahl and Dickens

1 Compare the letters of Charles Dickens and Roald Dahl and make notes on the differences between them. Use a grid like this:

	Roald Dahl	Charles Dickens
• the world he lives in	rail travel	aircraft
• his personality		
• language and tone of letters		
• the way he recounts dramatic events		

2 Both Dickens and Dahl became famous writers. What other similarities can you find in the two sets of letters? In pairs, compare the way in which each writer:

- uses dialogue to bring his account to life
- gives vivid details
- includes exciting descriptions of dramatic moments and incidents
- expresses his personal feelings
- varies the tone of his writing, so that he can be, for example:
  - light-hearted
  - matter-of-fact
  - dramatic
  - concerned.

Comparing letters

1 Which of the letters in this section did you enjoy most? Talk about your favourites in small groups, giving reasons for your choices. You might have chosen a particular letter because:

- it was dramatic, vivid, amusing . . .
- you found the subject-matter interesting
- you enjoyed the language

or for any other reason.

2 Pick your favourite letter in this section and write a reply to it. You could choose to be Henry VIII, for example, writing back to Anne Boleyn, or Mrs Dahl writing to her son in hospital. (Lady Hamilton, unfortunately, would have heard of Nelson's death before receiving his letter.)

You will need to pick up points in the original letter. To give you some ideas, here is a list of the recipients of some of the letters, with a sentence that each one might want to use as their main point, when writing their reply, together with a suggestion about the main tone or tones they might use:

Recipient	Possible sentence in their reply	Main tone(s) they might use
Molyneux	I did not open your letters!	hurt; resentful
Carlisle	I'm sorry I haven't written, but . . .	apologetic
Ireton	I am not a traitor . . .	angry; defensive
Stella Campbell	Knowing what you feel about the war I understand your anger . . .	calming; explaining

Recipient	Possible sentence in their reply	Main tone(s) they might use
Henry VIII	You ask that you should be the only one to be punished . . .	hard; not giving in
Sam's father	Will you still be able to use a plough . . .?	practical; proud
President Roosevelt	This is indeed worrying news . . .	concerned; urgent
Irma's sister	I have no idea whether you will ever receive this letter	sad; loving
Maclise	Sorry to hear about the Raven . . .	amusing
Mitton	Thank goodness you are safe . . .	relieved; anxious for more news
Mrs Dahl	There are a few details you have missed out . . .	suspicious and concerned

3 Most of the letters in this section were written by people who lived in earlier centuries, some as far back as the sixteenth century (the 1500s). Think of a person from history who interests you (someone who is no longer alive) and write a letter from them to a friend or enemy. You could choose someone from the distant past (such as Shakespeare), or a more recent figure (such as Diana, Princess of Wales).

Think carefully about the tone that you should adopt and the kind of language you might use. If you are feeling confident, you might try to imitate the language of someone like Dickens or Sidney, if your writer comes from that period. Here are some well-known historical figures who come from roughly the same periods as the pre-1900 writers in this section. Some are found in other parts of this book.

Historical period	Writers in the section	Other people from that time (some of them are in other sections in this book)
1500s & 1600s	Anne Boleyn Sir Philip Sidney	Sir Thomas More Queen Elizabeth I William Shakespeare
1700s & 1800s	Nelson Sam	The Duke of Wellington Jane Austen
1800s	Charles Dickens	Charles Darwin Mary Seacole Chief Joseph Abraham Lincoln
1800s & early 1900s	George Bernard Shaw	Emmeline Pankhurst Robert Falcon Scott

Section 5
SPEECHES

You only have to look at a stirring performance of Shakespeare's Henry V as he cries 'Once more unto the breach, dear friends!' or Mark Antony calling out 'Friends, Romans, countrymen! Lend me your ears' to realise what power a good speech can have. Each of the speeches in this section had a major lasting effect on its hearers; and they are worth reading today, not just because of their historical importance, but also for their brilliant use of language.

Martin Luther King

On 28 August 1963, a quarter of a million demonstrators gathered in the American capital, Washington DC, to protest for 'Jobs and Freedom'. They were addressed by the black civil rights leader Martin Luther King. Although he had planned what to say the night before, it took only one look at the vast army of listeners for him to decide that most of the speech should be improvised. What he said led to changes in government policy; and King's moral leadership brought him the Nobel Peace Prize the following year. He began, in words which have become justly famous the world over, with a statement of his vision of the future.

I have a dream that my four little children will one day live in a nation where they will be judged not by the color of their skin but by the content of their character. I have a dream, today! I have a dream that one day, down in **Alabama**, with its vicious racists, with its governor having his lips dripping with the words of **interposition** and **nullification**, that one day right there in Alabama, little black boys and black girls will be able to join hands with little white boys and white girls as sisters and brothers.

He concluded, emotionally, with many of the crowd in tears:

Let freedom ring. And when this happens, when we allow freedom to ring, when we let it ring from every village and hamlet, from every state and every city, we will be able to speed up that day when all of God's children – black men and white men, Jews and Gentiles, Catholics and Protestants – will be able to join hands and sing in the words of the old Negro spiritual, 'Free at last, free at last; thank God almighty, we are free at last.'

A year later the Civil Rights Bill was made law. In 1968 King was in Memphis, Tennessee and told his audience: 'I may not get to the promised land with you, but I want you to know tonight that we as a people will.' The next day he was assassinated.

Alabama: one of the main centres of racism
interposition: interference
nullification: cancellation

Sir Winston Churchill

In the summer of 1940, Britain was in a desperate situation in its war with Nazi Germany. The Prime Minister, Sir Winston Churchill, knew that a morale-boosting speech was what the country needed, and this is what he said to a packed House of Commons on 4 June:

We shall not flag or fail. We shall fight in France, we shall fight on the seas and oceans, we shall fight with growing confidence and growing strength in the air; we shall defend our island, whatever the cost may be; we shall fight on the beaches, we shall fight on the landing grounds, we shall fight in the fields and in the streets, we shall fight in the hills; we shall never surrender.

Churchill's inspiring words did much to strengthen people's resolve during the dark days of the Second World War. He continued in politics until 1964 and died a year later.

Our freedom and our land

Since the earliest days of the cinema, countless films have been made showing the conflict between 'cowboys' and 'Indians'. Usually the cowboys won. Only recently have films such as *Geronimo* begun to tell the story from the native Americans' point of view. In fact, there were many great native American leaders in the nineteenth century who spoke out powerfully in defence of their people's freedom. In these extracts, two chiefs express their feelings about the land that is being snatched from the native Americans and about their loss of liberty.

Tecumseh

Tecumseh was a Shawnee warrior who tried in vain to stop Indian territories being taken over by the white settlers. In 1810, the Governor of Indiana Territory, William Henry Harrison, had signed a treaty with some of the older and weaker chiefs as a result of which the tribes lost their land. Here is part of a speech in which Tecumseh rejected this treaty.

I am a Shawnee. My forefathers were warriors. Their son is a warrior. From them I take my only existence. From my tribe I take nothing. I have made myself what I am. And I would think that I could make the red people as great as the conceptions of my mind, when I think of the Great Spirit that rules over them all. I would not then come to Governor Harrison to ask him to tear the treaty. But I would say to him, Brother, you have liberty to return to your own country.

The way, the only way to stop this evil, is for all the red men to unite in claiming a common and equal right in the land, as it was at first, and should be now – for it never was divided, but belongs to all. No tribe has a right to sell it, even to each other, much less to strangers, who demand all, and will take no less.

Sell a country? Why not sell the air, the clouds and the great sea, as well as the earth? Did not the Great Spirit make them all for the use of his children?

Tecumseh's vision came to nothing, for, by 1855, a treaty had been signed which forced all native Americans into reservations.

Chief Joseph

Many fought on, however, and one of the last was Chief Joseph, leader of the Nez Perces. But in 1877, after a long pursuit by the American army which ended in a siege lasting five days, Chief Joseph accepted that all was lost. This is part of his famous surrender speech:

Tell General Howard I know his heart. What he told me before, I have it in my heart. I am tired of fighting. Our chiefs are killed. Looking Glass is dead. Toohoolhoolzote is dead. The old men are all dead. It is the young men who say 'yes' or 'no'. Ollokot, he who led the young men, is dead. It is cold, and we have no blankets. The little children are freezing to death. My people, some of them, have run away to the hills, and have no blankets, no food. No one knows where they are – perhaps freezing to death. I want to have time to look for my children, and see how many of them

I can find. Maybe I shall find them among the dead. Hear me, my chiefs! I am tired. My heart is sick and sad. From where the sun now stands I will fight no more forever.

Two years later, Chief Joseph was allowed to address the American President in Washington, asking that his people might be allowed to return to their homelands in the cool, mountainous north-west. His stirring words were different from what the hushed audience had expected to hear from an 'Indian':

There has been too much talk by men who had no right to talk. Too many **misrepresentations** have been made, too many misunderstandings have arisen between white

misrepresentations: false accounts or representations

men about the Indians. If the white man wants to live in peace with the Indian, he can live in peace. There need be no trouble.

Treat all men alike. Give them all the same law. Give them all an even chance to live and grow. All men were made by the same Great Spirit Chief. They are all brothers.

You might as well expect the rivers to run backward as that any man who was born free should be contented penned up and denied liberty to go where he pleases.

Let me be a free man – free to travel, free to stop, free to work, free to trade where I choose; free to choose my own teachers, free to follow the religion of my fathers, free to think and talk and act for myself – and I will obey every law, or submit to the penalty.

In 1885, Chief Joseph and other exiles were permitted to return to the north-west; but they were never allowed to go back to their homeland in Oregon, and the Chief died in 1904, reportedly of a broken heart.

Abraham Lincoln

In the nineteenth century, America was torn apart by a civil war between the Unionists of the North and the Confederate South. This is the famous speech made in 1863 by the American President, Abraham Lincoln. Named after the battlefield in which the Confederates were defeated, it is known as the Gettysburg Address.

Fourscore and seven years ago our fathers brought forth on this continent a new nation, conceived in liberty, and dedicated to the proposition that all men are created equal.

Now we are engaged in a great civil war, testing whether that nation, or any nation so conceived and so dedicated, can long endure. We are met on a great battlefield of that war. We have come to dedicate a portion of that field as a final resting-place for those who here gave their lives that that nation might live. It is altogether fitting and proper that we should do this.

But, in a larger sense, we cannot dedicate – we cannot **consecrate** – we cannot **hallow** – this ground. The brave men, living and dead, who struggled here have consecrated it far above our poor power to add or detract. The world will little note nor long remember what we say here, but it can never forget what they did here. It is for us, the living, rather, to be dedicated here to the unfinished work which they who fought here have thus far so nobly advanced. It is rather for us to be here dedicated to the great task remaining before us – that from these honored dead we take increased devotion to that cause for which they gave the last full measure of

consecrate: set apart as sacred   **hallow**: honour as holy devotion; that we here highly resolve that these dead shall not have died in vain; that this nation, under God, shall have a new birth of freedom; and that government of the people, by the people, for the people, shall not perish from the earth.

Lincoln had great plans for healing the wounds of the civil war, but he did not live to carry them out. He was assassinated by a supporter of the South only two years later.

Elizabeth I

In August 1588 England was threatened with invasion from Spain. As the terrifying Armada (war-fleet) of Spanish ships sailed up the English Channel, Queen Elizabeth arrived at Tilbury to address her troops. Thousands had gathered to see her and many of her advisers were concerned for her safety. There might, after all, be Spanish assassins in the crowd. This is how she brushed off their fears.

My loving people! We have been persuaded by some that are careful of our safety, to take heed how we commit ourselves to armed multitudes for fear of treachery. But I do assure you, I do not desire to live to distrust by faithful and loving people. Let tyrants fear! I have always so behaved myself that, under God, I have placed my chiefest strength and safeguard in the loyal hearts and goodwill of my subjects. Therefore, I am come amongst you as you see at this time, not for my recreation and **disport**, but being resolved, in the midst and heat of the battle, to live or die amongst you all – to lay down for my God and for my kingdoms, and for my people, my honour and my blood even in the dust! I know I have the body of a weak and feeble woman, but I have the heart and stomach of a king, and a King of England too; and think foul scorn that Parma or Spain, or any Prince of Europe should dare to invade the borders of my realm, to which, rather than any dishonour should grow by me, I myself will take up arms.

disport: pleasure

By your obedience to **my General**, by your **concord** in the camp and your **valour** in the field, we shall shortly have a famous victory over these enemies of my God, of my kingdoms and of my people!

The Spanish Armada was scattered and destroyed, and Elizabeth went on to rule an increasingly powerful England for a further fifteen years.

---

my General: the Earl of Leicester
concord: disciplined behaviour
valour: courage, bravery

ACTIVITIES

Martin Luther King

King's speech was so powerful, not just because of what he said, but because of the way he said it. If possible, watch or listen to a recording of King, and you will hear the power of his voice and his dramatic delivery (you can hear a few lines on Encarta).

You can see that King begins his speech with specific personal points and moves towards the idea of freedom for all black people. He also uses the following techniques:

- repetition
- vivid description (e.g. of the Governor of Alabama)
- emotive words (e.g. 'little', 'sisters and brothers')
- building up an idea (village, city . . .)
- pairings (black men and white men . . .)
- quotation.

Find examples of each of these techniques in the speech.

As a class, discuss why you think these are effective. Are some more effective than others? Why?

Sir Winston Churchill

1 How can you tell that these words were spoken, not written? Talk together about Churchill's use of:

- repetition ('we shall . . .')
- 'place words' to remind people that it is their country they must defend ('island . . . beaches . . .')
- a powerful concluding statement.

How many times does he use the word 'we'? Why do you think he decided to repeat it so often?

2 If possible, listen to a recording of Churchill making a radio broadcast. He emphasises particular words and phrases, and also pauses for effect in places. What comes across from a recording which it is impossible to get from just reading the text?

3 Imagine that Churchill had wanted to put these same points into a letter. Redraft the speech as part of a letter to one of his generals who had been suggesting that they were facing defeat. You might begin:

> We are not going to give in. First of all we still have some troops in France, which can . . .

Compare the original speech with the letter you have written. What are the main differences that you notice?

Tecumseh and Chief Joseph

One of the central beliefs of the native Americans was that nobody had a right to 'own' the land: it had been created by the Great Spirit and had always been shared; they simply could not understand how the white settlers could claim whole areas of territory as their property.

1 Pick out the most powerful statements from the three speeches which express the idea that:

- nobody has a right to 'own' the land
- the white settlers are greedy
- the native Americans have had enough of war
- all men have a natural desire to be free
- people should be free to do as they wish, so long as they obey the law.

2 Imagine that you are a television director, making a party political broadcast with Chief Joseph, based on his speech beginning 'Tell General Howard . . .' (page 147). You decide to illustrate the Chief's speech with powerful images.

a) Jot down the key pictures that the Chief conjures up in his speech (the dead chiefs, the cold, the freezing children . . .)

b) Think about how you want the audience to feel at different points in the speech, and make notes on this.

c) Then, using your notes from **a)** and **b)**, write an artwork brief for the series of images which will make up the broadcast. There should be shots of the Chief as well as the key pictures. Include some of the Chief's words to accompany each of the images. If you prefer, you could sketch a series of frames, to make up a storyboard for the broadcast.

Abraham Lincoln

Lincoln's speech has been very cleverly put together. He has clearly thought very seriously about the message he wants to get across and has taken great care over the structure and the choice of language to convey a particular tone.

1 Copy this grid and fill in the third column by finding as many examples as you can of the language features listed in the second column. Some examples have been included to start you off.

Structure feature	Language	Examples
1 The speech is in three sections • Section 1: *the past*, indicated by • Section 2: *the present*, indicated by • Section 3: *the future,* indicated by	verbs in the past tense verbs in the present tense verbs in the future tense	**brought**
2 The sections are linked • He links the whole speech by	repetition of words	**conceived**
3 Sentences are balanced • He makes his points in an effective way – e.g. by	grouping phrases in threes	**we cannot dedicate**
• He creates a memorable final statement – e.g. by	repeating the phrase but changing the preposition (of, by . . .)	

2 If you listen to the language used, you can hear a number of different tones. Four of these tones are listed in the grid below, together with the language Lincoln uses to get them across to his audience. Fill in the third column with examples of this language.

Structure feature	Language	Examples
Optimism – suggested by	the adjective 'new'	
Patriotism – suggested by	adjectives such as 'great'	
Unity – suggested by	pronouns ('we', 'us', 'our')	
Firmness – suggested by	short statement sentences	

3 As a class, talk about why you think the Gettysburg Address became so memorable and important for the American people.

Queen Elizabeth I

1 Queen Elizabeth I knew exactly what she had to say at Tilbury in order to raise her forces' spirits. Select the moments in her speech where she manages to get across the idea of:

- her own bravery
- her trust in her people
- her willingness to share the fate awaiting her people
- her courage and resolve
- her expectation that the English forces will behave in an ordered and disciplined way
- her belief that she has God on her side.

Which of her statements do you think would have got the biggest cheers from the assembled crowd?

2 Imagine you are a Spanish spy at Tilbury. Write a letter back to your superiors in Spain, in which you report Queen Elizabeth's speech and express your opinion on it. You could mention some of the examples you picked out for activity 1. You might start off:

> Dear Don Andrea,
> This woman is a more powerful enemy than we had thought . . .

Comparing the speeches

1 What similarities can you find between all these speeches?

a) Draw a grid like the one below, and put a tick under the speaker's name if you think that his or her words convey the message in the left-hand column.

Messages	Martin Luther King	Sir Winston Churchill	Tecumseh	Chief Joseph	Abraham Lincoln	Elizabeth I
we have powerful enemies						
but we must never give in						
we are patriotic and love our country						
we should stand together and remain united						
we can trust our people to remain strong						
things will get better						
we must defend our freedom						

b) Which speaker has been most successful in getting particular points across? Find your favourite examples and then decide which speech was the most effective overall, in your opinion.

2 Write your own speech to deliver to the rest of the class. Think of something about which you feel really strongly. You could use some of the techniques you have learned about in this section, such as:

- repetition (Martin Luther King and Churchill)
- vivid description (King and Chief Joseph)
- emotive words (King and nearly all the other speakers)
- structure (Lincoln).

You might include examples of some of the messages that you picked out in activity 1.

Section 6
NELSON MANDELA:
ONE MAN – MANY STORIES

Through his fight against apartheid (the system which oppressed black people) and his leadership of the new South Africa, Nelson Mandela has become one of recent history's great figures. In this section you can read accounts of his life from a wide variety of different sources. To begin with, there is an overview from an encyclopedia on CD-ROM; following that, his early political life is reported in a history book for young readers. A newspaper article deals with Mandela's trial by the South African authorities as an alleged terrorist; and you can read Mandela's own account of his time in prison, from his autobiography, *Long Walk to Freedom*. Finally, Mary Benson's biography reports the moments surrounding Mandela's release and his first words as a free man.

These five accounts have been written with different audiences in mind. Each one tells a different part of Mandela's story, so that, taken together, they provide a snapshot history of one of the greatest leaders of modern times.

His life in a page

This article is from the CD-ROM encyclopedia Encarta. It is aimed at a wide audience of all ages who might want a quick overview of Mandela's life.

Mandela, Nelson Rolihlahla (1918–), South African activist, statesman, and **Nobel laureate**, who was elected the first black president of South Africa in 1994. Mandela rose to national prominence as the leader of protest against the white minority government's policy of rigid racial segregation known as apartheid, which officially ended in 1991. Elected president in the country's first democratic elections, Mandela promised a new multiracial government that would work to reverse the economic and social problems caused by apartheid.

Mandela was born as the son of Tembu tribal chief in Umtata, in what is now the province of Eastern Cape. He became a lawyer, and in 1944 joined the African National Congress (ANC), a civil rights group, and helped establish the organisation's Youth League. In 1956 Mandela went on trial for treason, but was acquitted in 1961. During this time he married Nkosikazi Nomzamo Madikizela (*see* Mandela, Winnie); they separated in 1992 and divorced in 1996. In the early 1960s Mandela led the ANC's paramilitary wing, Umkhonto we Sizwe ('Spear of the Nation'). Arrested again in August 1962, he was sentenced to five years in prison. While in prison, Mandela, along with several others, was convicted of sabotage and treason and in June 1964 was sentenced to

Nobel laureate: someone who has won a Nobel Prize

life imprisonment. During this period Mandela became a worldwide symbol of resistance to white domination in South Africa. The government, under Present F. W. de Klerk, released Mandela in February 1990 after lifting the ban on the ANC. Mandela assumed leadership of the ANC and led negotiations with the government for a new constitution that would grant political power to the country's black majority population. In 1991 the government repealed the last of the laws that formed the legal basis for apartheid. Mandela and de Klerk shared the 1993 Nobel Peace Prize for their efforts in establishing democracy and racial harmony in South Africa. In May 1994, after the country's first multiracial elections, Mandela became president of South Africa.

Early years

This extract is from *Life Stories*, a series written with younger readers in mind. It takes us from Mandela's days as a university student through to his arrest in 1955 and the notorious Treason Trial. (Mandela was convicted and went to jail, but was acquitted in 1961.)

Nelson's best friend at university was Oliver Tambo, who was another black law student. In 1944, Nelson and Oliver helped to start a group called the Youth League. This was part of an older organisation called the **African National Congress (ANC)**, which was working to get better treatment for black people in South Africa. By 1949, Nelson and the Youth League had taken control of the ANC.

However by then, life for blacks in South Africa had got worse because the **government** wanted to separate black people and white people completely. Its word for this was **apartheid** (pronounced 'a-par-tide').

Nelson and the other ANC leaders hated apartheid because it meant that blacks could not live in certain areas, could not vote, and could not use the same services as white people. So they organised strikes, boycotts and other protests. They broke apartheid laws and held noisy public meetings all over the country. The police often attacked them and there was a lot of violence. In 1952, Nelson was put in charge of these public protests for all of South Africa. He also became head of the ANC in Transvaal, the rich area which included Johannesburg.

Then the government arrested Nelson because he was a danger to its rule. It used one of the worst apartheid laws against him and '**banned**' him. This meant that Nelson could not attend any public meetings, could only meet one person at a time, and was watched closely by the police the whole time. Nelson was a prisoner in his own home.

Three years later, in 1955, Nelson went to a big **rally** near Johannesburg. It was a very important rally because it was held by the Congress Alliance. This was a new organisation which was the first group to include both black people and white people. Nelson went to the rally in disguise because he was still banned by the government and was not allowed to go.

The Congress Alliance scared the government because it was more dangerous to its rule than the ANC. So Nelson was arrested again at the rally, along with 155 others. They were all put on trial which dragged on for four and a half years. This trial was called the Treason Trial.

Trial for terrorism

This newspaper article is from 1962, when Mandela was once again facing trial by the apartheid regime.

Nelson Mandela, man of courage

In Johannesburg today the case is due to open of the State v. Mandela. Undoubtedly the court will be crowded out with supporters of the resistance movement, just as it was in 1952 when 13 African and Indian leaders, including Mandela, were tried for organising the great Defiance Campaign against unjust laws, and again in 1956 when 156 men and women, including Mandela, were accused of high treason. Others have written and will write more fully about Nelson Mandela's life. These are the personal impressions of one of his friends which may add something to the portrait of this remarkable African nationalist.

As I have grown to know Mandela, the qualities that have struck me most have been a combination of authority with gentleness, of **militant** dedication with gaiety, of generosity with daring. For some time after I first met him, about nine years ago, however, I saw him simply as a tall, handsome, rather 'slick' young man, and even when I worked alongside the accused people during the first year of the treason trial, although I liked him, I still did not take him very seriously. It was when I started researching for my book on African leaders and sought opinions from people of all races throughout South Africa that I began to take notice, and my own increased knowledge of him confirmed what I was told.

INTERESTING AND EXCITING

Several of the eminent lawyers involved in the treason trial defence gave me their impressions of the trial. Mandela's name recurs in my notes of those interviews:

'If one had to pick someone who won the case, then I would say Nelson Mandela … He said we want to squeeze these people (the Government) until they give in. He was not afraid.'

As for these men's individual opinions of Mandela, one said: 'A most impressive man with real political intelligence'; and another: 'Articulate, a remarkable man.'

Then over and over again, not only from them but from an uncommitted academic,

militant: showing willingness to fight

from an **ambivalent** newspaper editor, from Indian leaders who had known Mandela since 1944, and from his own colleagues and followers, came a predominant impression of how over the years he has grown.

So many men understandably grow negative or shrivel up and retreat in face of the prolonged persecution and frequent setbacks as they pit their strength against the tyrannical might of the armed South African state. But Lutuli and Mandela are among the leaders who were undeterred, indeed stimulated, by such factors.

Nelson Mandela told me something about his home during the series of talks that we had – it was in a Tembu **kraal** of thatched, white-faced huts by the Bashee River, a green-watered stream flowing through the lovely hills of the Transkei. He recalled a picture of 'beautiful vegetation, fine stock, plenty to eat,' and he was delighted when I was able to drive through this valley, now bare but still beautiful. Considering the perilous life he was leading underground, it was comic to think that as a boy he had felt his life to be dull and **circumscribed**, and envied his more **plebeian** friends who boasted about their exploits, such as stealing a pig, and taking it to the forest to kill and roast and eat.

ambivalent: having mixed feelings
kraal: village of huts, enclosed by a fence
circumscribed: limited
plebeian: working-class

Another comic picture that he re-created was his arrival in the fabulous city of Johannesburg, where he – an aristocrat, by the way – briefly became a mine policeman, sitting at the gate of the compound, clutching his 'badges' of office – a whistle and a **knobkerrie**! And his ambition, at the time, was to become a clerk in the Native Affairs Department. We laughed a lot, too, at his first experience in human relations with Europeans – when the lawyers to whom he was **articled** were not keen to use a new, inexperienced typist, so she asked Mandela for work and he would dictate to her, until one day while he was doing so a European client came in and she, clearly worried at being seen taking dictation from a native, pointedly asked, 'Do me a favour, Nelson; go down to the chemist and buy me a shampoo,' thus re-establishing the 'proper' master/servant relationship.

Mandela's greatness was apparent in things that he told me about his children, and also in his attitude to human beings and creatures in general; his generosity was apparent in his comments on the most **virulent** of the former-ANC's rivals; his authority is in his bearing and his dedication runs through his life.

His warmth and gaiety are delightful to

knobkerrie: short stick with a knobbed head
articled: apprenticed
virulent: extremely hostile

experience and in the midst of tension he can be at once reassuring and fun. Though he never took risks needlessly, his daring filled one with **trepidation**.

He told me a story of one narrow escape some months ago: a friend was due to pick him up on a street corner when the split-second timing essential to secrecy broke down through friends being caught in traffic jam. As Mandela stood there he suddenly felt someone watching him, turned and to his utter dismay saw a non-white policeman staring at him with obvious recognition. He was waiting for the tap on the shoulder that preceded arrest when the policeman moved towards him, gave the illegal ANC thumbs-up sign, murmured 'Afrika!' and strolled away!

Now that Mandela has been captured by the forces whom he brilliantly eluded for 15 months, of one thing we can be sure: he and his wife Winnie will show the same blazing courage and selflessness that have so moved all of us who are proud to be their friends.

August 16, 1962.

trepidation: fear, alarm

Imprisonment

After the trial, Mandela was sentenced to imprisonment on Robben Island, notorious for its harsh conditions. Here he picks up the story himself (in his autobiography, *Long Walk to Freedom*) and describes his arrival on Robben Island and some of the treatment he had to suffer.

We were driven to the old jail, an isolated stone building, where we were ordered to strip while standing outside. One of the **ritual indignities** of prison life is that when you are transferred from one prison to another, the first thing that happens is that you change from the garb of the old prison to that of the new. When we were undressed, we were thrown the plain khaki uniforms of Robben Island.

Apartheid's regulations extended even to clothing. All of us, except **Kathy**, received short trousers, an insubstantial jersey, and a canvas jacket. Kathy, the one Indian among us, was given long trousers. Normally Africans would receive sandals made from car tyres, but in this instance we were given shoes. Kathy, alone, received socks. Short trousers for Africans were meant to remind us that we were 'boys'. I put on the short trousers that day, but I vowed that I would not put up with them for long.

The warders pointed with their guns where they wanted us to go, and barked their orders in simple one-word commands: 'Move!' 'Silence!' 'Halt!' They did not threaten us in the swaggering way that I recalled from my previous stay, and betrayed no emotion.

ritual indignities: everyday humiliations   **Kathy**: here, a man's name

The old jail was only temporary quarters for us. The
authorities were in the process of finishing an entirely
separate maximum-security structure for political
prisoners. While there, we were not permitted to go
outside or have any contact with other prisoners.

The fourth morning we were handcuffed and taken in
a covered truck to a prison within a prison. This new
structure was a one-story rectangular stone fortress with
a flat cement courtyard in the centre, about one hundred
feet by thirty feet. It had cells on three of the four sides.
The fourth side was a twenty-foot-high wall with a catwalk
patrolled by guards with **German shepherds**.

The three lines of cells were known as sections A, B, and
C, and we were put in section B, on the easternmost side
of the quadrangle. We were each given individual cells on
either side of a long corridor, with half the cells facing the
courtyard. There were about thirty cells in all. The total
number of prisoners in the single cells was usually about
twenty-four. Each cell had one window, about a foot
square, covered with iron bars. The cell had two doors:
a metal gate or grille with iron bars on the inside and
a thick wooden door outside of that. During the day, only
the grille was locked; at night, the wooden door was
locked as well.

The cells had been constructed hurriedly, and the walls
were perpetually damp. Many mornings, a small pool of
water would have formed on the cold floor overnight.
When I raised this with the commanding officer, he told
me our bodies would absorb the moisture. We were each
issued three blankets so flimsy and worn they were
practically transparent. Our bedding consisted of a single
sisal, or straw, mat. Later we were given a felt mat, and
one placed the felt mat on top of the sisal one to provide

German shepherds: alsatian dogs   **sisal**: a rough fibre

some softness. At that time of year, the cells were so cold and the blankets provided so little warmth that we always slept fully dressed.

I was assigned a cell at the head of the corridor. It overlooked the courtyard and had a small eye-level window. I could walk the length of my cell in three paces. When I lay down, I could feel the wall with my feet and my head grazed the concrete at the other side. The width was about six feet, and the walls were at least two feet thick. Each cell had a white card posted outside of it with our name and our prison service number. Mine read, 'N Mandela 466/64,' which meant I was the 466th prisoner admitted to the island in 1964. I was forty-six years old, a political prisoner with a life sentence, and that small cramped space was to be my home for I knew not how long.

That first week we began the work that would occupy us for the next few months. Each morning, a load of stones about the size of volleyballs was dumped by the entrance to the courtyard. Using wheelbarrows, we moved the stones to the centre of the yard. We were given either four-pound hammers or fourteen-pound hammers for the larger stones. Our job was to crush the stones into gravel. We were divided into four rows, about a yard-and-a-half apart, and sat cross-legged on the ground. We were each given a thick rubber ring, made from tyres, in which to place the stones. The ring was meant to catch flying chips of stone, but hardly ever did so. We wore makeshift wire masks to protect our eyes.

On one of our first days pounding rocks, a warder commanded Kathy to take a wheelbarrow filled with gravel to the truck parked by the entrance. Kathy was a slender fellow unused to hard physical labour. He could not budge the wheelbarrow. The warders yelled: 'Laat daardie kruiwa loop!' (Let that wheelbarrow move!) As

Kathy managed to nudge it forward, the wheelbarrow looked as if it would tip over, and the warders began to laugh. Kathy, I could see, was determined not to give them cause for mirth. I knew how to manoeuvre the wheelbarrows, and I jumped up to help him. Before being ordered to sit down, I managed to tell Kathy to wheel it slowly, that it was a matter of balance not strength. He nodded and then carefully moved the wheelbarrow across the courtyard. The warders stopped smiling.

The next morning, the authorities placed an enormous bucket in the courtyard and announced that it had to be half full by the end of the week. We worked hard and succeeded. The following week, the warder in charge announced that we must now fill the bucket three-quarters of the way. We worked with great diligence and succeeded. The next week we were ordered to fill the bucket to the top. We knew we could not tolerate this much longer, but said nothing. We even managed to fill the bucket all the way, but the warders had provoked us. In stolen whispers we resolved on a policy: no quotas. The next week we initiated our first go-slow strike on the island: we would work at less than half the speed we had before to protest at the excessive and unfair demands. The guards immediately saw this and threatened us, but we would not increase our pace, and we continued this go-slow strategy for as long as we worked in the courtyard.

Robben Island had changed since I had been there for a fortnight's stay in 1962. In 1962, there were few prisoners; the place seemed more like an experiment than a full-fledged prison. Two years later, Robben Island was without question the harshest, most iron-fisted outpost in the South African penal system. It was a hardship station not only for the prisoners but for the prison staff. Gone were the Coloured warders who had supplied cigarettes and sympathy. The warders were white and overwhelmingly **Afrikaans**-speaking, and they demanded a master-servant relationship. They ordered us to call them 'baas', which we refused. The racial divide on Robben Island was absolute: there were no black warders, and no white prisoners.

Mandela was to remain in prison on Robben Island for 28 years.

Afrikaans: the language of the hard-line Dutch settlers in South Africa

Release

At long last the apartheid regime crumbled and Mandela was released in February 1990 to become the first President of a free South Africa. His biographer Mary Benson describes the moment when he regained his freedom.

Sunday, 11 February 1990: a hot summer's day in the Cape. For the crowd waiting outside Victor Verster prison, and for the world watching on television, the expectation was thrilling. What would he look like, the world's most famous political prisoner who had been kept invisible from the public gaze for more than a quarter of a century? The man labelled a 'terrorist' by the government which was about to release him?

For hour after hour the people waited. The delay added tension to the expectation as eyes strained in the glare and television cameras focused on the prison gates. And then a motorcade of cars approached and from the leading car stepped Nelson Mandela. A tall, very slim and distinguished, elegantly suited man beamed as, with his handsome wife, he walked through the gates into freedom.

Mandela felt he had entered 'a totally different South Africa'. He was amazed at the friendly crowd which jostled to draw close and by the whites, smiling and waving to identify themselves with what was happening, who lined the roads along the thirty-five-mile drive to Cape Town.

On his arrival there, Mandela was escorted to the balcony of the City Hall. He was overwhelmed by the sight of eager, upturned faces filling the Grand Parade below. Raising a fist, he cried out, *'Amandla! Amandla! Mayibuye iAfrika!'* (Power! Power! Let Africa return!) Those slogans echoed with a roar before – with Cyril Ramaphosa, the mineworkers' leader, holding the microphone – he could continue: 'Friends, comrades and fellow South Africans, I greet you all in the name of peace, democracy and freedom for all. I stand here before you not as a prophet but as a humble servant of you, the people.'

Nelson Mandela was President of South Africa until his retirement in 1999.

ACTIVITIES

It is important to be aware of the different types of biographical information that can be found in various texts and different media. This section gives you the opportunity to study many stories about one man through five different sources.

His life in a page

The Encarta article is made up of two solid blocks of text. This is fine for a CD-ROM encyclopedia, where people need to print out a page and don't want to use up too much paper. But it does make it hard to read.

1 To gain a clearer idea of the facts of Mandela's life, convert the text into bullet points. Don't write out complete sentences, but just the main facts, dates and key words. For example, you might start off:

- born 1918
- activist . . .
- first SA president 1994
- rose as anti-apartheid leader . . .

2 a) Think about the areas of Nelson Mandela's life which are covered by the entry – personal details, political activity, imprisonment and so on. Now group the points as notes for paragraphs, and give each paragraph a topic heading. For example, the first paragraph might be headed 'Overview of Nelson Mandela's life'.

b) Have you kept the bullet points in more or less the same order, or have you moved them around to match the topic headings? Whichever you have done, what does it tell you about the Encarta entry? (A clue: find out what 'chronological order' means.)

Early years

Because this book was written as part of a school series, it takes care to explain a number of words and ideas which younger children might find difficult. Another way of explaining words is to put them in a glossary at the end of the book or at the bottom of the page as we have done in this book.

Find the following words and phrases in the extract, and then write a definition of each one to help younger children understand what it means.

• African National Congress (ANC) • government
• apartheid • strikes • boycotts • protests • 'banned'
• rally.

To start you off, here is the kind of explanation you might write for *government*:

> GOVERNMENT The people in charge of the country. The South African government at that time did not include black people.

Trial for terrorism

The article in the *Guardian* was written on the day that Mandela's trial was due to start. The writer focuses on the human qualities of the man, the 'personal impressions of one of his friends', rather than just his skills as a politician and leader.

1 a) What does she say about:
- the qualities she now knows he possesses (page 168 column 1)
- her early impressions (page 168 column 1)
- his courage as a lawyer (page 168 column 2)
- the opinions of the lawyers in the treason trial (page 168 column 2)
- his refusal to become negative (page 169 column 1)
- his background (page 169 columns 1 and 2)
- the sometimes amusing relationships with the lawyers to whom he was articled (page 170 columns 1 and 2).

   b) Which qualities does she go on to mention on page 170 column 2?

   c) What does the story on page 171 column 1 tell us about South African society at that time?

2 Look over your answers to activity 1. Can you summarise them as a list of the main human qualities which have caused so many people to admire Nelson Mandela? Compare your list with other people's and in pairs, talk about the qualities you chose. List three (or more) on which you both agree.

Imprisonment

This extract is from Nelson Mandela's autobiography, and so it contains his own memories and feelings about his time in Robben Island prison. Other people who were there at the same time, of course, would have their own impressions, because they saw things from a different viewpoint.

1 One of Mandela's fellow prisoners was Kathy, who shared the task of pounding rocks. Imagine that you are Kathy and write an extract from your autobiography about your time in prison. In particular, try to say:

- what qualities Mandela displayed when he
  - helped you cope with the wheelbarrow
  - organised the go-slow
- what your personal feelings were for the man.

In addition, you could write about

- how you felt about being the only Indian among the African prisoners
- how you felt about being older than the other prisoners
- the cell you were imprisoned in (the same as Mandela's)
- the agonising job of crushing stones (Mandela recalls that you were 'unused to physical labour')
- the problems you had with the wheelbarrow one day, and the help Nelson Mandela gave you
- the go-slow
- the prisoners' relationship with the white warders.

Release

Imagine you are making a television news programme about Nelson Mandela's release from prison. Using the information in Mary Benson's biography, write a commentary to accompany the following camera shots:

i	Camera 1 pans round the crowd waiting outside Victor Verster prison. Every now and then it focuses on the prison gates.
ii	A motorcade of cars approaches the prison gates from inside.
iii	Nelson Mandela steps out of the leading car with his wife and walks out through the gates
iv	People jostle to greet him; he talks to some of them and then gets back into the car, which drives off.
v	Camera 2 (in an open-topped car) follows the motorcade on its five-mile journey to Cape Town: shots of people lining the streets.
vi	He arrives at the City Hall, where thousands of people are waiting.
vii	Camera 3 shows him coming on to the balcony; we hear the chants of the crowd.
viii	Cyril Ramaphosa holds the microphone as Mandela speaks . . .

Comparing the texts

1 Work in groups of six. Each take a different text and make notes on the following questions:

- What medium is used (CD? book? newspaper? . . .)
- What are the main pieces of information given?
- Does the extract contain facts, or opinions, or both?
- Who is writing or speaking? Whose point of view is being given?
- What can you say about the language? (For example, is it formal or informal? Is it aimed at a particular audience – if so, which?)
- What tense is used?
- What do you think are the key features of your text? Do they make it different from some or all of the others? How? (For example, how can you tell that one of the texts is written for a young audience?)

2 Look at all the notes made by your group. What have you learned about Nelson Mandela as **a)** an important historical figure and **b)** a man with amazing human qualities? Look up the following sections to give you some ideas before you write an encyclopaedia extract on Nelson Mandela:

The Leader: ● His life in a page ● Early years ● Imprisonment ● Release.

The Man: ● Trial for terrorism ● Imprisonment.

To remind yourself about writing for an encyclopaedia, look back at the two entries on Marilyn Monroe (pages 19–21) and the activity on page 30.

3 Pick another well-known figure. Then decide on two different ways of writing a biography. For example, you might choose to write a newspaper article like the one from the *Guardian* in this section (pages 167–171), and an extract from a school history textbook.

To help you plan your work, look back at the step-by-step approach to writing a biography on pages 32–33.

When you write your final drafts, leave a wide column down one side of the page. Then add notes in that column to show the differences between the two extracts that you have written. Use the bullet points in activity 1 as a guide to the kind of thing you might comment on.

Acknowledgements

The Editor and Publishers would like to thank the following
for permission to use copyright material:

Extract from 'Lost in France' by Mark Palmer, published by Fourth Estate.
Copyright© 1998 Mark Palmer. Reprinted by permission of Fourth Estate Limited;
Extract from 'Ewan McGregor' by Brian Pendreigh. Reprinted by permission of
Orion Publishing Group Limited; Extract from 'Leonardo Di Caprio: Modern Day
Romeo' by Grace Catalano. Copyright© Grace Catalano 1997. Published by Bantam
Press, a division of Transworld Publishers. All rights reserved; Extract from 'Paul
McCartney: Behind the Myth' by Ross Benson. Reprinted by permission of Orion
Publishing Group Limited; Extract from 'Book of Black Heroes – Volume 2. Great
Women in the Struggle' published by Just Us Books Inc 1991. Reprinted by
permission of the publishers; Extracts from 'Encarta®' reprinted with permission
from Microsoft Corporation; Extract from 'Oxford Children's Book of Famous
People'. Reprinted by permission of Oxford University Press; Extract from 'Dickens'
by Peter Ackroyd, published by Sinclair Stevenson. Reprinted by permission of the
Random House Group Limited; Extract from 'Who On Earth is Tom Baker' by Tom
Baker, published by HarperCollins Publishers Limited. Reprinted by permission of
Harper Collins Publishers Limited; Extract from 'Three Singles to Adventure' by
Gerald Durrell. Copyright© Gerald Durrell 1954. Reproduced with permission of
Curtis Brown Limited, on behalf of the Estate of Gerald Durrell; Extract from
'Unreliable Memoirs' by Clive James, published by Jonathan Cape, reprinted by
permission of the Peters, Fraser & Dunlop Group Limited; Extract from 'Notes
From a Big Country' by Bill Bryson. ©Bill Bryson, published by Doubleday, a
division of Transworld Publishers. All rights reserved; Extract from 'Cider with
Rosie' by Laurie Lee, published by Hogarth Press. Reprinted with permission of the
Random House Group Limited; Extract from 'Robbie Williams: Let Me Entertain
You' by Jim Parton, published by Virgin Publishing Limited; Extract from 'The Diary
of a Farmer's Wife 1796–1797' by Anne Hughes (Allen Lane 1980) Copyright©
Mollie Preston, 1937, 1964, 1980. Reprinted by permission of Penguin Books
Limited; Extract from 'The Prose Works of Sir Philip Sidney', Albert Feuillerat.
Reprinted by permission of Cambridge University Press; Extract from 'Bernard
Shaw: Letter to Mrs. Patrick Campbell 7 January 1918'. Reprinted by permission of
The Society of Authors on behalf of the Bernard Shaw Estate; Extract from 'Voices
in the Night' by Marianne Elsey. Reprinted with permission of the author; Extract
'Out of Tune' by Geoffrey Watson©Geoffrey Watson, first published in The
Guardian; Extract from 'Mobile Madness' taken from Daily Mail 7.1.00. Reprinted
with permission of Solo Syndication Limited; Extract from 'Going Solo' by Roald
Dahl, published by Jonathan Cape & Penguin Books. Reprinted by permission of
David Higham Associates Limited; Extract from 'Charles Dickens Selected Letters'
ed. David Paroissen, published by Gale Group. Reprinted by permission of The
Gale Group; Extract from 'Martin Luther King' by Harry Harmer, published by
Sutton Publishers. Reprinted with permission; Extract from 'a speech made in the
House of Commons on 4 June 1940', Copyright Winston S. Churchill. Reproduced
with permission of Curtis Brown Limited, London, on behalf of the Estate of Sir
Winston S. Churchill; Extract 'Nelson Mandela: Man of Courage' by Mary Benson.
© The Guardian. Reprinted with permission; Extract from 'Long Walk to Freedom'
by Nelson Mandela. Copyright© 1994 by Nelson Mandela. Reprinted by permission
of Little Brown and Company Inc.; Extract from 'Nelson Mandela: The Man and the
Movement' by Mary Benson (Penguin Books 1986) Copyright © Mary Benson
1986. Reprinted by permission of Penguin Books Limited.

The Publishers have made every effort to trace the copyright holders, but if they
have inadvertently overlooked any, they will be pleased to make the necessary
arrangements at the first opportunity.

The best in classic and

Jane Austen

Elizabeth Laird

Beverley Naidoo

Roddy Doyle

Robert Swindells

George Orwell

Charles Dickens

Charlotte Brontë

Jan Mark

Anne Fine

Anthony Horowitz